1939 – Dundee at War

Like many other parts of Scotland, Dundee had suffered during the Depression of the 1920s and 1930s with the jute industry upon which the city depended being particularly hard-hit. Shipbuilding also suffered, along with a number of other minor industries. The inter-war years had been very hard for Dundee with the traditional industries upon which the city depended being badly affected especially jute and shipbuilding. In the worst years of 1931–1932 over 70 per cent of those previously employed in the jute industry were unemployed. The coming of the war led to a turn-around in both industries; shipbuilding orders took off while the massively increased requirement for sandbags led to a similar recovery in the jute industry.

One of the first jobs at the Caledon Yard was the refitting of two Polish submarines. The *Orzel* and the *Wilk* had managed to escape from the Baltic, despite the attempts of the German and Russian forces, and made for Britain. As Dundee was a major submarine base the yard was the obvious location for the repair and refitting operation to be carried out. The *Orzel* (Eagle) was a modern vessel that had been commissioned in 1939. Damaged by German minesweepers, she had put into the neutral Estonian port of Tallinn. Here, her commanding officer had gone ashore to be treated for an illness and, under German pressure, the Estonians boarded the submarine, interned the crew and set about removing navigational aids and armament.

The crew, however, hatched a daring escape plan and on the night of 18 September they overpowered their guards, cut the mooring lines and set off. The submarine, running half-submerged, was fired upon and ran aground on the bar at the mouth off the harbour. While grounded she was hit and damaged by artillery fire which destroyed her wireless equipment. The crew managed to re-float her though and set course for Britain, after hearing that the Polish submarine *Wilk* had managed to escape to Britain. The crew put the two captured Estonian guards ashore in Sweden with money and new clothing before setting off across the North Sea. With almost no navigational aids the new commanding officer of the *Orzel* used a list of lighthouses to find the east coast of Scotland. Lying on the bottom, repairs were made to her wireless and she broadcast a message in English which resulted in a destroyer being sent to escort her.

Attitudes towards the possibility of enemy bombing varied widely in Dundee. There was, of course, the commonly held fear which was shared up and down Britain, but there was also a widespread belief that Dundee would be spared the attentions of the Luftwaffe because the electors of the city had not returned Winston Churchill to office in the 1922 General Election. Churchill's bitterness and anger towards the city as a result were well known, as was the fact that he had vowed never to return to Dundee.

One of the first real signs of war coming to Dundee was when the city's evacuation plan was initiated on 1 September. On this first day some 8,800 children and mothers were removed from home to a number of locations in Angus and the Mearns. On this first day children from sixteen schools were evacuated. Evacuees from the more outlying schools were ferried to Union Street by trams and buses and from there they marched in an orderly fashion to the Tay Bridge and East Stations. Mothers carrying young infants were assisted through the queues and helped teachers to care for the children, who all carried their kit in parcels and suitcases along with their gas masks.

The Director of Education, Mr John Cameron, who had the unenviable task of being in charge of the evacuation, told the press that it had gone as smoothly as could be expected and reports from the reception areas showed no problems in finding suitable accommodation. This was largely due to the fact that the numbers that had turned up were far

YOUR TOWNS & CITIES IN WORLD WAR TWO

DUNDEE
AT WAR 1939–45

YOUR TOWNS & CITIES IN WORLD WAR TWO

DUNDEE
AT WAR 1939–45

CRAIG ARMSTRONG

Pen & Sword
MILITARY
AN IMPRINT OF PEN & SWORD BOOKS LTD.
YORKSHIRE – PHILADELPHIA

First published in Great Britain in 2021 by
Pen & Sword Military
an imprint of
Pen & Sword Books Ltd
Yorkshire – Philadelphia

ISBN 978 1 52670 468 9

A CIP catalogue record for this book is
available from the British Library.

Typeset by SJmagic DESIGN SERVICES, India.
Printed and bound by CPI Group (UK) Ltd, Croydon, CR0 4YY

Pen & Sword Books Limited incorporates the imprints of Atlas, Archaeology,
Aviation, Discovery, Family History, Fiction, History, Maritime, Military, Military
Classics, Politics, Select, Transport, True Crime, Air World, Frontline Publishing,
Leo Cooper, Remember When, Seaforth Publishing, The Praetorian Press,
Wharncliffe Local History, Wharncliffe Transport, Wharncliffe True Crime and
White Owl.

For a complete list of Pen & Sword titles please contact
PEN & SWORD BOOKS LIMITED
47 Church Street, Barnsley, South Yorkshire, S70 2AS, England
E-mail: enquiries@pen-and-sword.co.uk
Website: www.pen-and-sword.co.uk

Or
PEN AND SWORD BOOKS
1950 Lawrence Rd, Havertown, PA 19083, USA
E-mail: Uspen-and-sword@casematepublishers.com
Website: www.penandswordbooks.com

Contents

smaller than had been expected and which had turned up during the rehearsals. One woman, however, clearly saw the benefits and jokingly turned up to one of the evacuation centres, telling the officials that she was not part of the evacuation, but asking if she could go with them for the weekend! On the following day a further 13,123 were expected to leave the city.

In the event, fewer children left than expected and by the time the evacuation had been completed on Saturday afternoon, 2 September some 17,200 children and mothers had left the city. Many others, of course, had made private arrangements and the sum of evacuees was in fact higher than the official figure. At Kirriemuir the evacuees from Dundee were welcomed by local Territorials and marched to the hall where a large crowd assembled to greet them and take them to their new homes. Despite the official line that the children were

Dundee evacuees arrive by bus at East Station. (Dundee Evening Telegraph)

all calm and orderly, the reality was that a great many were anxious and upset over the upheaval which saw them wrenched from their families and familiar surroundings and deposited in an unknown place amongst strangers. Worse still, not every billeting area was pleased to receive them.

Montrose had seen 2,542 children and mothers sent from Dundee and had managed to billet 1,827 of these. The authorities in Montrose were angered that larger towns, such as Arbroath, had received fewer evacuees from the city, but it would seem that the real reason was rather more sinister. A meeting of the Montrose Town Council held on 11 September saw heated debate, with Councillor Butchart protesting vociferously against the arrangements which had been made. He told the meeting that an excessive number had been sent to the town and that 'the condition of many of the children, indicated neglect on the part of the responsible authority in the sending area'.[1] The councillor concluded by saying that there was no need to go into details about the condition of the children as most of the council had direct experience. The Provost of Montrose contacted the authorities in Dundee to complain about the matter. He noted that this was not a criticism of Dundee, but he had a duty to the people of Montrose who had been badly let down.

As the preparations for the war continued there was an ever-increasing demand for added protection for important locations throughout the city and outskirts of Dundee. Extra building work was undertaken to strengthen some structures, while a great many other locations received sandbagging protection. The need for sandbags was not confined to Dundee and the demand resulted in a revival of the badly flagging jute industry which in turn acted to relieve some of the unemployment problem in the city. The need for sandbag protection locally also resulted in a rush in the coastal community of Broughty Ferry. ARP personnel, volunteers and labourers from the Corporation and from private companies thronged Broughty Ferry beach to obtain sand with which to fill the ubiquitous sandbags.

Harris Academy evacuees heading for Brechin. (Dundee Courier)

Dundee evacuees at Kirriemuir awaiting further instructions. (Dundee Courier)

Part of the constant stream of lorries to collect sand from Broughty Ferry beach. (Dundee Courier)

The first Hogmanay of the war was expected to be a quiet one with several factors mitigating against the traditional celebrations. The first of these was the blackout, but the fact that New Year's Eve also fell on a Sunday and so licensed premises would be closed was also expected to be a significant factor. Chief Constable Neilans had ensured that the ban on the sale of fireworks was rigidly enforced. In the event the celebrations were indeed very low-key. The tradition of thousands gathering in High Street to see in the year was abandoned and there were no seething crowds to be seen, with Reform Street being described as being as quiet as a Sunday morning. Only in Overgate was there any real attempt at festivities, but even here they fell flat and the crowd was only of a size similar to a pre-war week-night. Those young people who did attempt to add some musical cheer usually did not progress beyond the first lines of a song before giving up as no-one joined in.

Some still engaged in first-footing, however, as the barrowmen who had earlier been selling cured red herring and imitation black puddings (both popular first-footing gifts) had done a fair trade. The lack of late tram cars and buses, however, encouraged many to stay at home during this first wartime Hogmanay, and although a crowd gathered in City Square to see in the New Year, the celebrations were very muted compared to those held in peacetime.

CHAPTER 2

1940 – ARP, LDV and Home Guard

Hogmanay also resulted in several minor criminal incidents. A taxi driver, Mr David Shand Stockman of 114 Seagate, was fined the sum of £4 and banned from driving for three months after he had been found guilty of operating a motor car while under the influence of drink. Mr Stockman had begun work on what turned out to be a busy Hogmanay and had at first turned down the repeated offers of drink from his customers, but as the night wore on he began to accept these offers. He was later called to Thorter Row but his fare did not turn up and Mr Stockman went to a nearby police box to ask the two policemen there if they had seen the fare. The officers quickly noticed that the taxi driver was drunk and arrested him. In sentencing Mr Stockman, the deputy procurator fiscal, Mr George A. McKenna, called the offers of drink 'stupid generosity' and appeared rather sympathetic to his case, saying that 'such misguided generosity on the part of his fares placed a very great strain on the taxi driver, having continually to refuse drinks which he was probably rather tempted to take'.[1]

An unfortunate consequence of the war was that there had been a growth in anti-alien feeling which was particularly directed against the Italian community in Scotland. Many Italian families had lived in the country for years and were firmly nationalised, with some even having sons serving in the forces, but the ill-feeling continued to cause problems. The New Year saw a group of men, most of them the worse for drink, entering a fish restaurant at 204 Perth Road. The owner of the business was an Ella Paladini. A quarrel subsequently arose and a stand-up fight between the customers saw tables and chairs overturned and damaged. The police were called and when they arrived all but two of the men ran off. These two men, Robert Downie Reid and Colin

Johnstone Leslie, both of 105 Hawkhill, were brought before Dundee Police Court and fined the sum of 10s apiece with the option of seven days' imprisonment.

The rapid formation of the ARP organisations led inevitably to problems and resentments. The controller in Dundee, under government orders, had recently set about reducing the number of full-time paid wardens and by the start of the year sixty-eight posts had been removed. Even this did not go far enough for some, however, and one letter-writer to the *Dundee Evening Telegraph* expressed the view that further reductions and alterations were required. The anonymous writer, who signed himself as 'Go Ahead', asked if the controller was aware that a number of the male wardens who were left were earning extra money through pensions or income in addition to the £3 or more weekly rate that they were paid for being wardens. He said that some of these men could, in the name of patriotism, resign their positions to become unpaid part-time wardens so that unemployed men could become paid wardens. After all, argued the writer, the job demanded only average intelligence and common sense and, downplaying the role, asserted that 'When, if ever, a real raid takes place, the work saving and helping to save life won't be confined to ARP personnel only. All patriotic citizens will be expected to rally to their aid.'[2]

Dundee Town Council met on 4 January to discuss the continuing closure of schools. The schools had been closed at the start of the war due to fears of immediate bombing and many had also been taken over by the ARP organisations for use as rest centres or first aid posts. Feelings ran high in Dundee over the continued closures, but a proposal that a public meeting be held to protest the closures was defeated by nineteen votes to eleven. There was evidence that parents were growing increasingly anxious and local efforts to re-open some of the schools had been vetoed by the government. Mrs Lily Miller argued that the continued closures were down to a lack of backbone on the part of Earl de la Warr and Kenneth Lindsay on the Board of Education and Department of Education for Scotland respectively and their failure to stand up to the Ministry of Health. Surely, she argued, if thousands of children in Dundee could attend cinemas, church and Sunday schools, they could attend school under the control of a teacher.

One of the main reasons for the continued closure was the fact that before a school could reopen it had to be furnished with an air raid shelter. Treasurer Caldwell moved an amendment and argued that, while he agreed that the schools should now be open, a public meeting would serve no purpose. Many of the school air raid shelters were now being built and it had been promised that schools would begin to reopen from mid-January. Convenor Wilson argued that the situation had been worsened by the failure of the evacuation scheme which had seen some 90 per cent of Dundee evacuees return to the city from safer areas, placing greater strain on any potential reopening.

The meeting also discussed the recent dismissal of full-time women ARP wardens and Mrs Miller declared that women were entitled to the same treatment as men and that, if sixty-eight wardens had to be dismissed, it should be the most incompetent who were dismissed first rather than on the basis of gender. Mr Peter Gillespie argued that this decision was not theirs and fell to the members of the Emergency Committee, but Mrs Miller immediately retorted telling him that this did not mean that the council should be beholden to the committee for all time and that 'if the elected representatives were going to hand over these matters to the Emergency Committee and sit back and allow them to play the same game as Hitler – only it was the married women's jobs he attacked – then they were foolish.'[3] Replying to Mrs Miller, the ARP controller, Councillor William Hughes, stated that the government had ordered that Dundee cut down its warden strength to 250. These wardens had to operate sixty-six posts and this meant that they had to reduce the number of wardens on duty at a post from four to three. Although, in his experience, many women wardens were every bit as able as the men, and in some cases more able, the women were only permitted to work a maximum of forty-eight hours per week whereas a man was permitted to work seventy-two hours. This meant that the authorities had to take the decision that to make best use of the personnel available it was the female wardens who largely paid the price for this government order.

Many of the people of Dundee keenly followed the fortunes of ships that had been built locally. The Caledon Yard produced several vessels which led interesting wartime lives. The SS *Arbroath*, a coaster built in 1935, was, like many vessels, commandeered by the Royal Navy in 1940. It was used during the Norwegian campaign and played a key role in the evacuation of personnel from Tromso. She then spent several years supplying the Allied garrison on Iceland and, following the D-Day landings in 1944, she was used to ferry supplies to the Mulberry Harbours.[4]

On the morning of Tuesday 9 January people in Dundee were awoken by the sound of explosions out to sea. A force of Luftwaffe bombers had attempt to bomb the Firth of Tay but had been detected by radar and British fighters were scrambled. The RAF fighters were spotted by the bombers while they were still some way from their target and the Luftwaffe aircraft immediately turned tail and fled, with some aiming bombs at a Trinity House lightship and a merchant vessel. Neither of the vessels was damaged and there were no casualties. The RAF fighters failed to make contact with the enemy due to the haze at the time.

The early weeks of 1940 had seen an outbreak of vandalism and thefts targeting air raid shelters in Dundee. A number of electric lamps had been stolen and switches destroyed in the attacks which had taken place across the city but were concentrated in the centre. The police took an extremely dim view of these selfish actions, cautioning the culprits that the shelters were kept open at night for a serious reason and that the consequences of missing or damaged equipment during an air raid could be severe. One policeman, interviewed by the press, was more blunt in his opinions, telling the reporter that 'If we get hold of the culprits they are for it.'[5]

As we have already seen, there had been some considerable criticism of the lack of preparedness for aerial attack on Dundee and on

7 February Dundee's Emergency Committee was stung into action and promised to construct public surface shelters at a cost of £100,000. One of the main problems was that many of the people who would be entitled to an Anderson Shelter lived in tenement buildings and so did not have gardens in which to erect them so these were to be for the use of the many residents who, although entitled to a free Anderson Shelter, did not have the ground to construct them. The shelters were to be erected at the back of tenement buildings and in those areas of slum clearance and would accommodate a total of 40,000–50,000 people. The money was reclaimable from the government in the form of grants.

There was something of a stir in February when four German airmen who had been shot down into the North Sea and picked up in their dinghy were brought initially to Dundee. They were the first of a small number of enemy airmen to transit through the city. The people of Dundee, and Britain, had yet to face serious bombing and there was not a great deal of hostility displayed towards these men. Indeed, they were viewed more as a curiosity than wartime enemies.

The rash of accidents that had occurred due to the blackout continued through the dark months of the winter and early spring. On 1 March four-year-old Hugh Crammond was knocked down by a vehicle in West Port. Hugh, of 219 Overgate, Dundee, died of his injuries three days later in Dundee Royal Infirmary.

Despite the labour shortages the unemployment situation remained in Dundee. The city had suffered chronic unemployment before the war and this situation was slow to resolve itself. By mid-March there were still 7,865 unemployed registered in the city. This had fallen by 693 from the previous month. The main changes in unemployment levels were in the Jute industry where the number had decreased by 311 (2,899 were still unemployed in this industry), the building industry where the number had decreased by 313 (376 were still unemployed), shipbuilding where the number decreased by 48 (172 were still unemployed), and engineering where the number decreased by 21 (102 remained unemployed).

Throughout the war people were urged to make do and mend and to make use of items which they might otherwise have thrown away. With farmers urged to plough up massive additional amounts of their land and to increase mechanisation in the industry, one Balgay Hill farmer came up with an ingenious solution in April. Mr David Robertson discovered and purchased a scrapped lorry and with considerable ingenuity, and at a cost of just 7s, re-purposed the apparently useless vehicle for service as a tractor on his farm.

As we have already seen, the slow construction of school air raid shelters had significantly delayed the reopening of schools in the city and when the Secretary of State for Scotland, Mr John Colville, visited Dundee in early April the opportunity was taken to ask him to look into the matter of increased grants for construction of these shelters.

Tractor converted from scrapped lorry at Balgay Hill. (Dundee Courier and Advertiser)

Mr David Robertson. (Dundee Courier and Advertiser)

The Corporation also asked about the supply of timber to allow the completion of the construction of some houses. Mr Colville answered that he would look into the matter of increased funding for the shelters and would do his best regarding the timber, but the situation was very difficult given the shortage of building materials. Mr Colville was spending two days in Dundee and St Andrews to inspect the ARP preparations. He had been given a tour of the city during which he visited a first-aid post and a school, and he expressed his satisfaction that the city seemed to be getting on well with the reopening of schools which had shelter protection.

While Mr Colville visited Ashludie Sanatorium and Rossie Priory, his wife, accompanied by the Lady Provost, visited war cookery classes and a number of ambulance units. His visit also coincided with a meeting organised by the Lord Provost to discuss the formation of blood transfusion associations and Mr Colville gave his support to this initiative telling the assembly that blood transfusion was a key part of the war emergency arrangements.

The Spring Bank Holiday saw the wartime conditions and the official warnings urging people not to travel largely ignored in Dundee as large numbers flocked to the rail and bus stations to journey forth. The most popular destination was Edinburgh, but this was closely followed by those who took advantage of cheap offers to travel to Aberdeen or Glasgow. Former holiday favourites such as Pitlochry and the resorts that were on the Highland Line saw less brisk traffic. Many people also boarded buses to St Andrews or other Fife resorts and bus tours were especially popular.

With the situation in France and the Low Countries increasingly bleak, the government finally bowed to severe pressure and authorised the formation of what it called Local Defence Volunteers. These armed and (eventually) uniformed volunteers would act initially as spotters of parachutists and were not expected to take an aggressive role but static defences might be allowable. The government completely underestimated the enthusiasm for the new force. Anthony Eden broadcast on the BBC on the evening of 14 May and within minutes volunteers were presenting themselves at police stations to register their names.

The creation of the LDV was largely carried out in an ad-hoc manner and there was a great deal of confusion initially. Dundee was made part of an LDV zone along with Angus and part of Kincardineshire. By 24 May, however, Lieutenant Colonel Hew Blair-Imrie of Lunan,

Lt-Col Blair-Imrie (l) and Mr Sillars (r). (Dundee Courier)

Montrose, was appointed the zone commander for Angus, Kincardine and the city of Dundee, while Mr Duncan Sillars was appointed as group organiser for Dundee.

By the end of the month company commanders had also been appointed following the system of burghs and districts. The commanders chosen were generally men who had seen service during the First World War with a typical example being one of the Dundee commanders. Mr Donald Ross of 1 Yewbank Avenue, Broughty Ferry, was the sole partner in the architectural firm of Carver, Symon & Ross and came from Glasgow. He had served as a lieutenant in the Royal Engineers for four and a half years during the First World War and had also served in Ireland during The Troubles in 1920. The other Dundee company commanders were Mr D.E. Collier of 15 Fintry Place, Broughty Ferry and rector of Morgan Academy, and Mr C.H. Horswell of 10 Airlie Place, the secretary of the Dundee Wireless College. During the First World War, Mr Collier had been a corporal in the Royal Engineers for two years before being commissioned as a lieutenant in the Royal Garrison Artillery and had been awarded the MC in 1918. Mr Horswell had been in the City of Dundee Engineers at the outbreak of the First World War. He had been wounded in action three times and at the end of the war was Garrison adjutant at Düren, Germany with the Army of Occupation.

Platoon commanders were also appointed. There were nine platoons in Dundee originally. The commanding officers of the three Broughty Ferry platoons were Mr Alan Fraser of Stirling House, Craigiebarns Road, the managing director of Peter McIntyre Ltd, who had seen service in the First World War with the Royal Army Service Corps; Mr A.B. Ruthven-Gartands of Strathearn Road, a jute merchant who had served in France as a captain with the Argylls and Mr R.M. Lindsay of 4 Balgillo Crescent. He had served as an officer for four years with the Fife and Forfar Yeomanry and the Royal Field Artillery and ended the war as a captain. Two of the men, Fraser and Lindsay, were also former captains of the Forfarshire Cricket Club while Mr Lindsay had also captained Panmure Rugby Club.

As the LDV expanded in Dundee to form two battalions it absorbed a number of units which were formed in individual industrial works and in the departments of Dundee Council. Indeed, the 2nd Dundee Battalion had five companies which were works units.

Company	Firm
A	Caledon Shipyard
B	Corporation Gas & Electricity Depts & Baxter Bros, Jute Manufacturers
C	Corporation Transport Dept
D	Urquhart, Lindsay & Robertson Orchar Ltd (textile machinery manufacturers)
E	LMS & LNER

One of the reasons for the enthusiasm with which the creation of the LDV was met was the changing attitude which could be seen in Britain after the Germans had invaded France and the Low Countries. A new spirit of determination had replaced the lacklustre attitude which had often prevailed during the Phoney War period. Many men, a great proportion of them being old soldiers, had been eagerly awaiting the chance to do something. Service in the ARP organisations had not seemed particularly attractive for some who saw the duties as being too inactive and many had been hoping and, indeed, praying for such an opportunity to arise.

Press reports implied that much of the German success was due to sabotage and treachery undertaken by either Fifth Columnists or by the landing of parachute troops. Many of the old soldiers realised that they would be seen as too old to be brought into the regular forces but were adamant that they could certainly make a substantial contribution to a force which was largely static, but which would fulfil an active military role in the event of enemy landings. Of the initial Dundee recruits there were many who had served in the First World War; some had even put in 21 years' service in the Army and were equally determined that, despite their age, they could contribute. One of the first to put himself forward declared that he remained a good marksman and that he saw the LDV as a 'very essential service'.[6] Perhaps anxious that some might doubt the abilities of the LDV he added that he hoped people would quickly realise the value of the service comparing it to the slack attitudes which had been at first demonstrated towards the ARP services. There was overwhelming support for the scheme from such men, with the majority declaring that, even if never called upon, it was better to be prepared.

Although the common view of the LDV (later renamed the Home Guard), helped by 'Dads' Army', is of elderly, even decrepit, men blundering about with little idea, the reality was that the average age of LDV members was in the 30s. Many who were in reserved occupations still wished to play a role in the defence of their country if the invasion came, while younger men saw it as a useful way of obtaining military training. One of the most youthful of recruits on the first day was a lad of 17 who told the press that if the war went on for some time he intended to join the Army and wanted to do something useful in the meantime. He also saw the benefits of everyone being able to handle a rifle in the event of invasion.

The LDV were expected to integrate their contribution with the overall defensive plan for the city and wider area which was developed by the local regular commanders. An initial plan drawn up by the commander of Polish forces in the Dundee area, for example, saw a defence based around an outer perimeter formed by the Kingsway (the orbital dual carriageway around the city which was built after the First World War) and an inner perimeter at key strategic locations.

The activities of the LDV came in for some ridicule with the force being derided as old men playing at being soldiers and nicknamed 'Look, Duck and Vanish' by some who took delight in ridiculing its duties of reporting parachute landings to the regular forces. Others, however, saw the value but were aware of the possible negative effect on morale within the force due to the criticism and ridicule. Winston

Churchill, with his knack for belligerent titles, quickly persuaded the authorities to rename the force with the more positive-sounding title of Home Guard rather than LDV.

Some regular officers were more welcoming of the efforts of the Home Guard than others, but the mixed attitude towards the force and the occasionally blimpish mentality of some Home Guard commanders sometimes resulted in confusion or a waste of effort. The regular Army officer commanding 543 Coast Regiment, Royal Artillery, for example, had been training members of 'C' Company, 1st City of Dundee Battalion, Home Guard in the manning of artillery at Broughty Ferry. Despite some initial problems in finding sufficient numbers of men to man the loading teams, the others, including the gun layers and other specialists, were soon brought up to a high level of proficiency. The officer reported back to his superiors that all of the LDV men were very keen, but this act of initiative on the part of the regular Army was brought to a halt when the Home Guard zone commander found out and ordered it to stop as it was not the duty for which the Home Guard was intended.

Minor traffic offences seem to have been the focus of Dundee Police Court at the start of June with three people being fined for leaving their cars in High Street and Murraygate. The first man was a member of the LDV. Albert Thain, a builder of 1 Glamis Place, explained that he had left the car in an accessible location so that he could get to it at a moment's notice in the case of an emergency. Mr Thain admitted that he had left the car on Hugh Street for over an hour and a half and admitted two previous offences. In view of his explanation Bailie Low restricted the penalty to just 10s. Janie Robb of 76 Muirfield Crescent was fined 10s 6d for having left her car unattended in High Street for one hour and forty minutes. William Martin, a plumber, was fined 5s for leaving his car in Murraygate for forty minutes. John Fyffe Peters, a railway worker from 88 Rosebank Street, was fined 7s 6d for the crime of having failed to obey the traffic sign while on his bicycle at the junction of Panmure Street and Meadowside. As a result, he had been in collision with a van and suffered injuries to his ear and hand which had required him to stay in hospital for one night.

Despite the fact that the government had ordered the removal of sixty-eight wardens at the start of the war, the ARP services in Dundee were by now well below strength in all branches. It had been decided that there would be a far greater reliance upon volunteers and there was to be a further reduction in the number of paid personnel. One result of this was an appeal on 18 June for teachers to come forward and volunteer for ARP service. Councillor Lily Miller successfully put forward a motion that headteachers be asked to make a return of teachers who were willing to undertake these duties and said she was sure that almost all of the teaching profession would be prepared to do whatever was asked of them.

Dundee became the first target of a series of raids on Scotland when the Luftwaffe tried to bomb the city on 2 August. Damage was very limited and the local press reported derisively on the abilities of the Luftwaffe. The raid, however, punctured the beliefs of some in Dundee who had optimistically hoped that the city would be spared the attentions of the German bombers due to the fact that it had failed to re-elect Churchill in the General Election of 1922.

With the expected heavy air raids having not developed there was some controversy over the state of the city's air raid precautions. On 20 June Councillor William Hughes, the air raid precautions controller, told the press that the city was short of 900 volunteer wardens and that the shortage was appalling given the circumstances. This led to disgruntlement amongst some of the city's residents and at the beginning of August one such resident wrote to the *Dundee Courier* asking if it was now true that the vacancies had been filled, but also adding that many volunteers had filled in forms weeks ago but had never been contacted by the authorities. Signing himself as 'Wearied With Waiting', he added that if there was no longer a demand for wardens then the council would be better to tell people this so that they could volunteer in other capacities such as with the WVS or in aiding the door-to-door collection of salvage.

Other criticisms of the warden service included a lack of control over the equipment issued to them. Just days after the above letter had appeared, another was published criticising the service. The writer, signing him or herself as 'Not At All Clear', asked if the authorities had any control over the stock which had been issued to warden posts and their occupants. The writer went on to claim knowledge of former wardens retaining their equipment, including steel helmets and respirators, while new recruits were experiencing problems obtaining the same equipment. Surely, they asked, the quartermaster of the force should ensure that all equipment is handed back by those who were no longer serving as wardens.

In the same column was a letter from Ruth Balfour, the chair of the WVS in Scotland. The letter expressed gratitude that the WVS members in Dundee had been asked to provide volunteers to make up for the shortage of recruits to the warden service in the city. She urged women to step forward, reminding them that they would be expected to shoulder greater burdens as men were called up for military service or entered the Home Guard. The long immunity from serious attack may have had a dampening effect on enthusiasm for the warden service but with the south of England now being attacked the situation had changed. She also took the opportunity to ask that those Dundee residents who had access to an Anderson Shelter quickly ensure that the shelter was prepared and rendered fit for use. It had come to her attention that many people were suspicious of the shelters, believing that they would not work. Recent events in the south of England, she claimed, had disproved this. She suspected that many of the rumours responsible for eroding faith in the Anderson Shelters were the work of Fifth Columnists and expressed the hope that the citizens of Dundee would not continue to be taken in by the rumours spread by possible enemy agents.

The paranoia expressed in the above letter was relatively common. Most people remained phlegmatic, but fear and anxiety also led to many expressing views which were not proven and excited the general public. Another letter, from someone who honestly signed themselves as 'Anxious', claimed that the authorities had not taken into consideration the dangers of tarred road surfaces. The writer claimed that these were a huge fire risk and that 'one or two incendiary bombs would set them on fire for miles'.[7] Such blazing roads would set fire to crops and woodland but such a disaster, the writer claimed, could be averted by the placing of sand at frequent intervals alongside the roads.

This paranoia extended into a continuing hostile attitude towards enemy aliens. Despite the internment of enemy aliens there were still those who wished to go even further. One correspondent, Mrs T.M.B. Garden of Blairgowrie, wrote to the *Dundee Courier* asking if it were not possible to 'get rid of the thousands of German and Italian women and children and old men, now interned in this overcrowded land, and to ensure their staying out of it?' She advised that the property of these people could be sold off by the Town Clerks of each burgh and the money used to 'pay for the ship charges to transport them – not too luxuriously – to Gibraltar, whence buses and lorries could take them to the nearest Spanish port',[8] and then onward to Italy. She claimed that the presence of these aliens in Italy would somehow be an embarrassment for Hitler and Mussolini.

With the majority of the action (but by no means all) in the Battle of Britain taking place over the south of England it was vital that Fighter Command keep a strategic reserve in the north of the country to protect both northern England and Scotland and to provide relief to those squadrons exhausted by the more ferocious action in the south. Early August found 249 (Gold Coast) Squadron based at RAF Church Fenton in Yorkshire. The squadron had formed as a Spitfire squadron but had converted to the more numerous Hurricanes and became operational at the start of July. This re-equipping meant that pilots had to quickly adjust to the new aircraft which involved hasty training. The squadron was also being sent up at night to experiment with the use of the Hurricane as a gap-filling night fighter. In the early hours of 16 July, however, tragedy hit when Hurricane I (P2995) suffered an engine failure shortly after take-off and crashed and burned in Copmanthorpe

Wood near York. The pilot, Sergeant Alistair David Williams Main (22), the son of Mr and Mrs D.W. Main of Dundee, was killed instantly. Despite his youth and the fact that he had been posted to the squadron in late June, Sergeant Main was clearly a skilled pilot and had shared in the destruction of a Junkers Ju88 on 8 July.[9]

Many young Dundee men had seen the approach of war and had decided that the glamour of being a pilot in the RAF was the best way to serve. One of these was William Gordon Dickie (24) who had joined the RAF Volunteer Reserve (RAFVR) in January 1939 and been called up on 1 September 1939 before completing his pilot training and being commissioned as a pilot officer at 6 OTU. He was then posted to 601 Squadron on 8 June. Based at RAF Middle Wallop, the squadron was in the front-line and Pilot Officer Dickie scored his first victory on 7 July when he shared in the destruction of a Dornier Do18. On the morning of 11 August he took off as part of a patrol over the Channel, but the patrol turned into disaster for 601 Squadron when four of its Hurricanes failed to return. All four aircraft had been shot down by Messerschmidt Me109s and all four pilots, including P/O Dickie, had been killed.[10] He was the son of William Bruce and Euphemia Dickie of Dundee.

The war had caused many headaches for the local authorities and Dundee Town Council had been in the middle of proposing a ten per cent cut in the rent for council houses. The war had interrupted this and the matter had to be referred to the Court of Session and the Lord Advocate had stated that the matter would have to remain unresolved until after the war. The council therefore announced that rents would remain unchanged for the course of the war.

Sergeant A.D.W. Main. (unknown)

Pilot Officer William Gordon Dickie.
(unknown)

With additional ARP duties placed upon high-ranking police officers, it was also announced that, at the suggestion of the government, the salary of Chief Constable Neilans was to be increased from the current rate of £750 rising to £850 to a salary of £800 rising in £50 biennial increments to £1,000 and that the scale would be backdated to 1 January meaning that the Chief Constable was due some £121 in back pay and would receive £900 per annum as from April.

Attitudes towards women in the workplace continued in some areas to be poor and, although the wartime situation was changing this, many employers continued to cling to antiquated viewpoints, especially towards married women. The war had also seen many men employed by the Corporation either called up or volunteer for the services and it was realised that the shortage of manpower would have to be filled with women. Thus, the Corporation agreed that, on a temporary wartime basis, married women would be employed for their clerical services and also that any single female clerk who wished to get married would have to leave the service, although they could be re-engaged as temporary clerks without superannuation allowances.

Many of the young men who had joined the Army discovered that service life was not what they had expected. Private John Stewart (19) had joined the Cameronians while still underage and had been disappointed to find that underage soldiers were not eligible for overseas service. Because of this, he had deserted and gone on the run and ended up back at his home in Broughty Ferry. While there he had been living with Jennie Loftus (or Bain), a married woman whose husband was serving abroad. The couple were brought before Dundee Sheriff Court charged with having stolen a number of household items including clothing and a ring from the 7 William Street, Dundee, property of Jean Young. Miss Young had locked up the house, which had belonged to her recently deceased mother, but agreed to rent the property to the accused who gave the names of Mr and Mrs Stewart. Miss Young discovered the thefts when she visited the house and she then informed the police. The two had subsequently been apprehended while wearing some of the clothing and jewellery and continuing to pose as man and wife. Mrs Bain had been using her Army allowance to support Private Stewart during this time. Private Stewart's solicitor claimed that his client had committed the crime to try to get out of the Army, but the fact that he had previously been convicted of attempted housebreaking obviously went against him and Sheriff Malcolm sent him to prison for two months. Mrs Bain, who had not previously been in trouble, was placed on probation for a year on the condition that she resided with her father.

July saw the Fleet Air Arm return to Dundee when the old naval air station known as RNAS Dundee (or Stannergate) was reopened and named HMS Condor II. The station was to serve as a satellite to the station at Arbroath.

The warden service in Dundee ran into more trouble when there were moves to remove the Head Warden from the northern post. The wardens in this area were disgruntled by this and sixty of the voluntary wardens immediately threatened to resign *en masse*. Clearly this would lead to a serious weakening in the ARP service in this area and the authorities backed down and reached a settlement with the wardens.

Despite the early upturn in the jute industry at the beginning of the war, by the summer of 1940 orders were slackening. Heavy goods were still in demand (mainly on government contracts) but the press reported that outside of this there was very little business taking place with consumer confidence low, especially in relation to hessian cloth. Prices were uncertain due to this lack of demand and the trade in yarns was also very subdued.

By early August the harvesting season for one of the most valuable crops in the Blairgowrie area was coming to an end. The crop of raspberries had turned out to be better than expected, although the harvesting had been disrupted by a lack of labour which resulted in work continuing on Sundays throughout the season. One change was that a greater percentage of the crop was dispatched pulped rather than fresh. In the week leading up to 3 August the district dispatched 256 tons of pulped fruit and 113 tons of fresh fruit from Blairgowrie Station. This meant that the Blairgowrie district had dispatched by rail a total of 1,186 tons of raspberries, 807 tons of pulp and 379 tons of fresh fruit. This beat the 1939 total of rail trade by 58 tons, but in 1939 this had been composed of 910 tons of fresh fruit and 218 tons of pulp. In addition to these totals large quantities of the crop had also been sent off via road and there still remained a large amount of pulp in the pulping yards.

Not everyone was convinced that the raspberry crop had been as good as the above statistics indicated. At the beginning of August, the Reverend A. Wylie Smith of Bendochy had written a column in the *Dundee Courier* praising the bounty of the raspberry crop, but his fulsome tone was found by one raspberry grower to be overly optimistic. Signing him or herself as 'Unhappy Rasp Grower', the writer informed the paper's letter column that his information, which he claimed to come from a very reliable source, was that the crop was approximately 30 per cent short of expectations and that this was one of the reasons why the price was steadily climbing towards £50 per ton. He concluded by saying that if the 'state of the rasp crop is an "encouraging omen for the victory of our cause", then God help us!'[11]

The local National Farmers' Union (NFU) in the Blairgowrie district was determined to support the war effort in ways other than the production of food and as the raspberry harvest came to an end the branch was organising a free gift sale which was to take place in September to raise funds for the Red Cross and the St Andrew's Ambulance Association. The preliminary arrangements were made by the Blairgowrie branch and the Chamber of Agriculture and districts from Glenshee to Cargill and from Meigle to Caputh and Clunie were taking part.

It was not only the farmers who were eager to produce food for the nation. The people of the Dundee area largely took well to the Dig for Victory campaigns and many Dundee residents turned their gardens over to the production of vegetables and fruit while others took on allotments to provide food for family and friends. The campaigns had been designed to further encourage the view that everyone was in the war together and all were expected to contribute. At least one Dundee resident, however, was left appalled by what they saw as a lack of effort on the part of the residents of the Beechwood housing scheme. They had been impressed by the wide, tree-lined, streets but left angry by the gardens which they claimed were largely derelict and filled with rubbish. The writer, signing his or herself 'Get Busy', admitted that many residents had made an effort to beautify the plots, but insisted that the vast majority seemed to have no interest and asked that the Corporation intervene.

An increasingly common sight on the streets of the Dundee area were soldiers from abroad. The nations conquered by the Nazis supplied many, but even more came from the Empire. Canadian soldiers made up the largest contingent and one Canadian sergeant who was staying in Dundee with family members had an unusual story to tell: for Sergeant Sam Reid of the 1st Canadian Division this was his third war. Sergeant Reid was originally from Renfrew but had emigrated to Canada and had been married for 36 years. During the Boer War he had joined the Royal Scots Fusiliers out of a desire to see South Africa. After the war he had stayed in South Africa for a couple of years working in the building industry. It was after he returned from South Africa

Sergeant Sam Reid, 1st Canadian Division. (Dundee Courier)

to Scotland that he had decided to visit Canada; he met his wife there and decided to settle in the country. During his time in Canada he had worked for over twenty years for the Public Works Department of the Provincial Government of Ontario. In the First World War he had been a sergeant in the Royal Engineers and had been awarded both the Distinguished Conduct Medal (DCM) and the Military Medal (MM). When the current war broke out Sergeant Reid had decided to leave his wife, two sons and two daughters, and join up once more because he 'wanted to be in at the kill'.[12]

Other Dundee families were not as sanguine or fired-up about the war as Sergeant Reid. The fighting during the fall of France had led to a number of deaths of men from Dundee while the fates of others were unknown. Some families were still anxiously awaiting news of loved ones who had been posted missing or of whom there was no news. Mr and Mrs G. Sharp of 88 Byron Crescent, for example, found out in early August that their youngest son, Private Charles Sharp (30), of the Argyll and Sutherland Highlanders, had been confirmed as having been taken prisoner. Private Sharp, a pre-war regular soldier, had been called up as a reserve at the start of the war. He was at the time working as a linesman with the General Post Office (GPO) in Glasgow.

On 12 June the surrender of the 51st (Highland) Division in France resulted in consternation throughout Scotland. Amongst the battalions captured were the 1st and 4th Black Watch. A great many men from Dundee were present in the ranks of these two battalions while there were others who were present in other attached units. When it became known, the loss of the division was a severe blow to the morale of Scotland and the bewilderment and sense of loss was also mixed with some anger that the Scottish division had been sacrificed or abandoned. This was more muted than it otherwise might have been as the press was not given the full details, but news leaked out after men who had been more fortunate and had escaped returned home on leave.

Two men from Rattray who had enlisted in the Cameron Highlanders together had also been posted missing. Private William Pyott (30) of 37 Westfield Terrace, Rattray, and Private John McPhee (24) of Berrydale, Rattray, were both unmarried and had worked at Hillbarns Farm in Blairgowrie when they decided to enlist in November 1939. Before enlisting Private Pyott had worked on local farms and as a roadman for the County Council while Private McPhee had spent most of his working life at Parkhill Fruit Farm in Rattray. McPhee's family had a phenomenal military record. He was one of five brothers, all of whom were in the Army. In the Great War his father and seven of his brothers had served (seven of them in the Cameron Highlanders) and only three had returned; two were once more in the Army.

Other local men to be posted missing included Sapper David Simpson Fender (22) of the Royal Engineers and Sapper Robert Donnet (20) of the Royal Corps of Signals. Sapper Fender was from William Street in Blairgowrie while Sapper Donnet was from Commercial Street, Ladybank, and had been a telegraphist and sorter at Ladybank Post Office. Sergeant Christian K. Mitchell (35) was serving with the Black Watch when posted missing. He lived at 10 Court Street and had been in the regular Army for twelve years, seven of which had been spent in India, and was member of the regimental football team. Another keen footballer to be posted missing was Private William Kinnes but his mother at 8 Brown Street received a postcard from him explaining that he was a prisoner and was safe and well. Prior to the war he had been a player for Dundee Celtic FC. Another family to hear good news was that of Gunner Ernest Hubbert Smith, Royal Artillery. Gunner Smith had been adopted by Mrs McLaughlin of 27 Kinnaird Street while he was a baby and had previously worked at the Bowbridge Jute Works. Another of Mrs McLaughlin's sons, Francis, was a member of the Royal Army Service Corps and had been evacuated from Dunkirk.

One family who had already been touched by tragedy received the news that a loved one had been wounded in the fighting in France. Private William Cole (39) of the Black Watch had been wounded three days into the German offensive on 13 May. Private Cole had been a Territorial with five years' service and had been called up at the beginning of the war. He left a wife and son at 9 Moncur Crescent when he departed for war. The family was also mourning the loss of a 13-month-old daughter who had died in January.

Amongst those units attached to the 51st (Highland) Division as divisional troops was the 237th (City of Dundee) Field Company, Royal Engineers. The company was captured along with the majority of the division on 12 June but, like other units, it had suffered casualties during

Above left: Gunner E.H. Smith, Royal Artillery. (Dundee Courier)

Above right: Sergeant C.K. Mitchell. (Dundee Courier)

the bitter fighting. Sapper John Leonard Street (22) was killed on 28 May and Driver Robert Ewing (20), the son of George and Agnes Ewing, lost his life on 7 June. Lance Corporal William Vaughan was the 20-year-old son of William and Isabella Vaughan and such was the confusion of the final days of the division that when he was confirmed as having lost his life his parents could only be told that this had occurred between 11-14 June.[13]

Private William Cole. (Dundee Courier and Advertiser)

While many in Dundee were concerned about loved ones posted missing in France the efforts to support the war effort went on. Two young Dundee women, Anna Samson (19) and Sadie Gilchrist (21), both of Lamb's Lane, gave concerts and sold rags and paper on behalf of the Red Cross. The two enterprising young women raised the sum of £2 16s for the Murraygate branch.

The government was particularly keen to maintain morale amongst the civilian population and one way in which this could be achieved was to make sure that everyone on the Home Front felt that they were actively making a contribution to the national war effort. One result of this policy was the urging of the public to donate scrap, especially metals which they were told could be turned into aircraft production. Everywhere across Dundee iron railings were cut down while housewives searched for old pots and pans which could be converted into the fighters and bombers which would take the war to Germany. In fact, hardly any of the metal salvaged was of suitable quality to be used in aircraft manufacture, but as a morale-boosting scheme the collections were a complete success. By the first week of August Dundee Corporation's Cleansing Department had finalised its plans for the scheme in the city and householders were told to have their salvage piled on the pavement ready for ward-by-ward collections which began at noon.

With the Battle of Britain raging, almost every sizeable community in Britain was collecting for its own Spitfire Fund. Dundee's efforts seem to have lagged behind some others, however, with the fund only being launched in the last week of August, but by the start of September the total stood at £615. The first contributions consisted of one large donation of £100 and various smaller ones, many of which were raised by back-green concerts, sales of work and whist drives.

People across Dundee were having to adjust to the increased wartime security measures with frequent identity card checks being commonplace. On 2 September a young woman domestic servant fell victim to this increased security when she failed to produce her identity card at the home of her employer and then again two days later at the police station. The young woman's solicitor questioned the right of the police to enter a private dwelling for the purpose of asking to see an identity card but was told that it was permissible. The woman went on to explain that she was from Liverpool and in 1939 had been working for short periods in several places across England before travelling to Dundee in January. At the time when national registration had taken place she had been unable to give her address and therefore did not have an identity card. Sheriff Malcolm told her that anyone without an identity card at this time would be viewed as suspicious, but obviously felt some sympathy for the young woman as he allowed a continuance so that she could explain her situation to a national registration officer and obtain a card but warned her that she must remain in Dundee during this time.

The resentment against some of the paid wardens continued into September when a letter appeared in the *Dundee Evening Telegraph* relating how the unpaid volunteer wardens were expected to relieve their paid comrades for a spell of duty each night. They had to (or volunteered to) scrub out the warden post every Friday night despite the fact that they had just finished shifts at factories or housework during the day. Surely, the vexed writer asked, the paid wardens should be capable of undertaking such cleaning both by day and night.

The council in Dundee had been awakened late to the fact that the city was not best prepared for an air raid and was lacking public shelters in some areas. In September it was announced that a further thirty-three public shelters were to be built and, at the end of November, that another twenty-six shelters were to be erected in Wards 4, 5, 8 and 9.

Fatalities amongst local airmen continued throughout the year. On the evening of 17 September wireless operator/air gunner Sergeant George Warden Brown and his crew were on a training flight as part of their duties with 14 OTU when their Hampden I (P4311) lost an engine. The pilot attempted a crash-landing but the aircraft stalled and crashed at Gwendraeth Marshes in Carmarthenshire, killing all four of the crew. The 20-year-old airman, the son of Robert and Mary Brown of Dundee, was buried at Pembrey (St Illtyd) Churchyard where his parents added this inscription: IN LOVING MEMORY OF DEAR GEORGE. HE DIED THAT WE MIGHT LIVE.

With the wartime situation incredibly tense the people of Dundee and surrounding areas still required some relaxation and local sporting leagues played a role in this. On Saturday 21 September the final of the Dundee Bowling Association's tournament was played out between teams from Broughty Ferry and Maryfield. The match ended with Broughty Ferry being victorious by 116-104. In keeping with the patriotic feeling in the country the tournament was held in support of the Red Cross and raised the sum of £52 5s.

Although a military force, the Home Guard had developed a reputation for its members being willing to speak their minds, especially if they thought they were not being treated seriously. In October a letter appeared in the *Dundee Courier* from a correspondent signing himself as 'On Night Duty' which asked the HQ of Dundee Home Guard why they were being so slow in the procurement and issuing of greatcoats to Home Guards who were standing night duty. The writer claimed that all the other battalions had greatcoats apart from Dundee.

The Luftwaffe returned to Dundee on 25 September when bombs were dropped on the city. One exploded at the junction of Nesbitt Street and Dalkeith Road while another hit a cabbage field close to the Eastern Cemetery. There were no injuries and damage was limited to broken windows and railings and a burst water pipe. However, Scotland was the subject of a mini-blitz at the start of November and Dundee was raided on two consecutive nights by small forces of bombers. On 4 November some thirty bombers crossed the coast and attacked the east end of Dundee. One bomb fell in Baxter Park and the explosion resulted in a huge crater and a large amount of dirt and stone being thrown into neighbouring streets along with a tree which was hurled over 100 yards. At the Taybank Works on Arbroath Road some fifty or sixty women who were working the night shift had a miraculous escape. They had taken shelter in an underground trench which was on vacant ground at the back of the works. A bomb scored a direct hit on the trench but struck a brick wall above the shelter and this diverted some of the blast. The workers owed their lives to the fact that they had all crowded together in one end of the trench and this was the end which escaped the worst of the blast.

On the next night the Luftwaffe returned. A single bomber released seven high-explosive bombs which fell in a straight line across part of the city. The most badly damaged area was Rosefield Street where a tenement building was demolished and 64-year-old Mrs Mary Ann Laing became the first Dundee civilian to be killed. A further twenty people were injured during this incident and twenty-four families made homeless. Another death occurred at Briarwood Terrace when a bomb scored a direct hit on the house of the Reverend A.M. Moodie. The minister, his daughter and housekeeper were sheltering in the basement at the time and both the minister and his daughter were extricated by rescue workers but there was initially no sign of the housekeeper. Two hours later the body of 61-year-old Mrs Elizabeth Duncan Cooper (from 341 Clepington Road) was recovered from the wreckage.

In Marchfield Road Mr Alexander Nicoll, his wife, daughter and sister-in-law were making their way from their bungalow to the shelter on the back-green when a bomb exploded in the middle of the front garden. The front of the bungalow was completely demolished but Mr Nicoll was the only member of the family to be injured. Bombs also fell on Farrington Street but no-one was hurt here although there was property damage. At the Queen Victoria Works on Brook Street some 100 employees had a lucky escape after a bomb fell onto the works, while part of the city, including the Forest Park Cinema, was left in darkness after a bomb exploded on an electricity transformer on Forest Park Place.

Three weeks after the 5 November raid on the city there came an unexpected conclusion when an unexploded bomb was discovered at the Taybank Works. A bomb disposal team set to work recovering the bomb, which was six foot in length and three in diameter and weighed

Bomb damaged tenement at Rosefield Street. (Dundee Evening Telegraph)

2,200lbs. After recovering the bomb, the device was blown up at Lumley Den with the explosion shaking the surrounding district.

One of the undoubted attractions of the Home Guard for many men, especially those who had previously seen service, was the comradeship that being a member of such a force engendered. A key to the fostering of this comradeship was the social scene outside of hours of duty and most Home Guard units organised numerous events. On 29 November, for example, Platoon Commander A.B. Ruthven organised a dinner at Kidd's Restaurant for the men of his platoon. Major Duncan Sillars and Captain Alan Fraser were amongst the guests and a varied programme of entertainment was enjoyed, completed by some community singing.

Such events were relatively common and in December 'A' Company of Dundee Home Guard held a whist drive and dance at Gray's Rooms. A large number of members and friends turned out, with the wife of Mr C.H. Horswell, the company commander, presenting the prizes.

We have already seen how there was extensive criticism of the ARP and civil defence scheme in Dundee, and it is true that the authorities seemed to have been slow to act on occasion. On 30 December the Fire Brigade Committee met and agreed to recommend the doubling of the manpower of the regular brigade. This would entail the recruitment and training of a further twenty firemen. It was also agreed to recruit four motor cyclists as auxiliary firemen and to increase the number of adult messengers to sixty (from thirty-two). There was further evidence of confusion when the ARP controller, Councillor William Hughes, explained that free stirrup pumps which had been issued would be withdrawn if those who had been issued with them were not prepared to work as a team. Such measures would seem late in the day, given that the headline in the *Aberdeen Press and Journal* which carried news of the vote had as its headline a story of how the Luftwaffe had tried to destroy London with incendiaries, but even now there appears to have been hesitancy and the vote was not unanimous, only being approved by six votes to two.

CHAPTER 3

1941–1942 – A Long Struggle

Amongst the many voluntary duties which were undertaken by the members of the WVS was the distribution of ambulances and canteens which had been bought by the American Red Cross and donated to Britain. In January, the district representative of the WVS, the Countess of Elgin, formally handed over a mobile canteen to the controller of ARP, Councillor William Hughes. During the presentation in City Square the Countess described how the people of America had not waited to be asked once they knew that Britain was standing alone against the tyranny of the Nazis and that gifts from the American Red Cross had poured across the Atlantic. The people of America, she claimed, were particularly moved by the plight of British civilians targeted by German bombing and had provided clothing, food and a number of mobile canteens. She went on to describe how, during the blitz on London, mobile canteens such as these had gone out nightly to supply food and drink to those made homeless and to the ARP workers. This canteen, she declared, would henceforth be available to Dundee and the surrounding areas in the event of a raid, although she hoped that Dundee would continue to be spared.

Acknowledging the gift, Councillor Hughes thanked the generosity of the American Red Cross and said that this was the first time anyone in Dundee had seen such a piece of equipment. The Corporation, he explained, had been toying with the idea of converting one of its buses to be used as a large mobile canteen but after hearing of the value of the lighter and more nimble mobile canteens, such as the one which had been presented, they were revising their ideas.

Amongst the properties which were taken over by the authorities for official use was the Mathers Hotel which was commandeered by

American mobile canteen in Dundee. (Dundee Evening Telegraph)

the Admiralty. The hotel briefly became the home of seventy-five women from the WRNS. The hotel was then the only WRNS wireless telegraphy school in the country and the young women seem to have enjoyed their stay in the city although the W/T school was moved to Yorkshire in 1942.

Dundee's War Weapons Week aroused great interest and generosity. One of the many attractions which people flocked to see was the display of an enemy fighter, a Messerschmidt Bf109, which had been shot down and crash-landed in Britain. The aircraft was displayed in the City Square and people crowded around to see the damage which had clearly been done to the aircraft with its battered wings, fuselage and engine, along with its propellers which were bent backwards as a result of the crash-landing.

Some of the men who had joined the services were of less than pure character and there were a number of incidents of soldiers and other service personnel being involved in petty crimes. On 18 January, for example, three soldiers were tried at Dundee Sheriff Court having been charged with the theft of 925 cigarettes, some confectionary and £1 8s 7½d in money following a break-in at a shop at 14 Union Street, owned by Annie Anderson. Private Patrick McFeely admitted a previous conviction at Glasgow, Private Arthur Cummings admitted previous convictions at Glasgow and Wellingborough, while the third accused, Private Malcolm Morrison was making his first appearance before the court. Finding all three men guilty, the Sheriff fined McFeely and Cummings the sum of £1 5s each while Morrison was fined 15s for this first offence.

Preparations for possible air raids included advice on water supplies in the event of raids while the people of Carnoustie were visited by their local air raid wardens at the beginning of February and issued with earplugs which could be trimmed to fit. Along with the earplugs,

Messerschmidt Bf109 on display in Dundee as part of the War Weapons Week. (Dundee Evening Telegraph)

people were asked to keep the new equipment in their gas mask cases and were warned to have their gas masks with them at all times.

On 1 February Dundee launched its War Weapons Week with a mile-long procession of British and Allied forces, joined by a contingent from the civil defence organisations. There was massive enthusiasm for the campaign and over 40,000 people, many of them youths and children, turned out in the City Square and adjoining streets. Lord Provost Wilson took the salute in the square as several RAF bombers overflew the city dropping leaflets promoting the campaign. An ambitious target had been set with hopes being expressed that £3,500,000 might be reached, a total representing £20 per head of population. This target had been increased from the initial one of £2,000,000. In declaring the opening of the campaign, Lord Provost Wilson mentioned the traditional and ancient rivalry with Aberdeen, whose own War Weapons Week was to start the following week. The Lord Provost expressed the hope that Dundee would outshine its rival and maintain its third position in the cities of Scotland with regard to war savings. By the end of the first day the people of Dundee had raised £1,499,995.

The people of the city had rallied enthusiastically to the cause and the final tally came in at the outstanding total of £2,764,886. The vast majority of this was donated by large investors who had given some £2,411,327 of the total, or 88 per cent of the final figure. It was hoped that the total would rise further as it did not include sums donated through the Bank of England, those delayed in the post and the money donated through the city's schools. Treasurer G.F. Caldwell expressed the hope that some generously disposed citizens might come forward to take the total to the £3,000,000 mark, while Lord Provost Wilson praised the 'stupendous success of War Weapons Week',[1] stating that the total represented the equivalent of more than £15 per head of population.

Those Dundee seamen in the Merchant Navy were expected to hold themselves to high standards of professionalism during the war though

Crowds at the opening of Dundee's War Weapons Week. (Sunday Post)

many fell foul of wartime regulations governing the Merchant Service. At the start of February one Dundee seaman was charged with having absented himself from his ship without leave, delaying the vessel from sailing. Martin Cully, a ship's fireman, of 72 Church Street, pleaded guilty to the charge at Cupar Sheriff's Court. In mitigation he stated that he had been told by the other firemen aboard the vessel that he was a liability and would be better off leaving. Mr Cully took the men at their word and had absented himself. The Procurator Fiscal, Mr R.S. Henderson, argued that the matter was made more serious because the absence of Mr Cully had delayed the ship from sailing for some time. The Honourable Sheriff A.E. Grosset sentenced Mr Cully to twenty-one days' imprisonment.

The men and women of the fire service, both regular and auxiliary, may not have had to cope with the levels of bombing that had been expected, but their jobs were still risky and their lives endangered tackling blazes. On the night of 8 February a fire broke out at the boot and shoe factory of John Winter & Son at Carnoustie. Help was quickly summoned from Dundee, but one fire engine was involved in an accident with a bus on the way, thankfully without anyone being hurt. At the scene the crews found the back of the premises, which housed the soft leather cutting department and machine room, was well ablaze. The office workers, who despite the late hour were still in the front of the building, were quickly evacuated and the firemen began to tackle the blaze. Three firemen were sent up on to the roof to remove slates to allow water to be poured onto the fire, but a wall gave way and fell onto them. AFS fireman James Devine, of 3 Fullarton Street, Lochee, suffered severe head, arm and leg injuries while regular fireman James Fleming, of 56 Williams Street, suffered head injuries. Fleming had been a member of the brigade for just a week. The third man was uninjured. Both the injured firemen were taken to Dundee Royal Infirmary.

On the night of 12 February the Luftwaffe made an attempt to raid various places in Scotland and there was a sensation when a stricken German bomber crashed in Pitairlie Wood close to the village of Monikie, killing all five of the crew.

On consecutive nights beginning 13 March the Luftwaffe blitzed Clydebank with horrific consequences. For the people of Dundee these nights were remembered for the lengthy alerts which saw them in their air raid shelters for much of the time as the German bombers passed overhead on their way to the target. The first night saw the longest alert in Dundee when the sirens sounded at 10:10pm with the all-clear not being sounded until 2:25am; but the sirens went again at 3:30am in an alert which lasted for six hours. On the following night the people of Dundee were in their shelters from 9:25pm until 1:45am.

By 1941 the military authorities were increasingly open to the possibilities offered of freeing up regular Army units by using the Home Guard to man coastal artillery positions, but there were problems with training the Home Guard in sufficient numbers and with the volunteer nature of the force. Many battery commanders, however, advocated the use of Home Guard platoons to act as infantry defence for the coastal units. This allowed regular Army platoons to take on more demanding duties elsewhere.

The use of the Home Guard in manning or protecting coastal gun sites saw a mixed response from the Royal Artillery officers commanding such sites; some were suspicious of the volunteers' abilities while others eagerly welcomed and recognised the fact that this would release numbers of regular soldiers. The Royal Artillery major who was commanding at Broughty Ferry, and who had been foiled by the intransigence of the Home Guard zone commander in a local initiative in which he trained Home Guards in 1940, took advantage of the new attitude and quickly had men from the 1st City of Dundee Battalion on duty guarding his battery at night. The local Home Guard commander, in contrast to his zone commander, was enthusiastic about the change and was eager for his men to increase this aspect of their duties.

As we have already seen, not every soldier took to Army life. On Saturday 3 May a two-man escort from the Pioneer Corps arrived in Dundee from Wales to pick up and escort a deserter from their regiment to London. The escort consisted of Lance Corporal James Dunlop and Private Stephen Sheppard (38). The two men visited the police station where the accused man, Private John Fitzgerald of 24 Atholl Street, Lochee, was being held and stated that they wished to take the prisoner immediately despite the fact that they were not going back until that evening. The police advised that it might be better for him to wait in the cells until closer to the time of departure, but the escort overruled them with the prisoner agreeing to 'play the game'.[2]

Lance Corporal Dunlop thought that it might be good for the accused to be able to visit his wife and three children, but the three men also took in a football match and visited three public houses, consuming six drinks each. They then went to Tay Bridge Station to catch the 8:37pm train. The lance corporal left the prisoner with Private Sheppard and went to get their tickets but while he was away Private Sheppard shot Private Fitzgerald dead.

Private Sheppard was initially charged with murder, but this was reduced to culpable homicide. The case was heard at Dundee High Court on 10-11 June. Lance Corporal Dunlop reported that when he had left the two men at the station he had told Private Sheppard to take no nonsense from the prisoner and to fire if necessary. The NCO denied that they were drunk and that the prisoner was not too drunk to try to escape. Indeed, the escort had been warned that Fitzgerald was a slippery customer, and it seems that he had been misbehaving as the day went on. Under cross-examination the lance corporal stated that Private Shepherd had told him that Fitzgerald had attempted to escape and had taken no notice of a command to halt before he had shot him.

Four witnesses were called by the prosecution, two of them railway employees. Hoistman James Stalker of 13 Sandeman Street testified that he thought Private Fitzgerald was 'pretty stotty' and that he seen him moving away from his guard saying, 'I'll play the game, I'll play the game,' while waving his hand. The guard put his rifle to his shoulder and fired, causing the deceased to fall against a barrow. Mr Stalker added that he thought that the prisoner could have been detained without shooting him.

Andrew Smith, a parcel porter, of 19 Peddie Street, testified that he heard the accused report to the Lance Corporal Dunlop that he had told the deceased he would do it 'and I have done it'. Petty Officer William Arthur Peck stated in his testimony that he had seen the accused standing with his rifle in hand after the shooting and heard him remark, 'He has been asking for it all day.'[3] Lance Corporal Thomas Gray of the Military Police stated that the accused smelled of drink but was quite capable of carrying out his duties. Lance Corporal Dunlop, on the other hand, had been reported for having been drunk on duty.

On the second day of the trial the defence brought forward several witnesses. One of the accused's officers, Captain Turner, testified that he had known Private Sheppard for a considerable time and that he was a most competent man and a very good soldier. He also clarified that there were at the time no guidelines stating that a guard should not shoot if a prisoner attempted to escape.

In his own testimony, Private Sheppard described how he had joined the Pioneer Corps as a volunteer in October 1939 and had served in France prior to the evacuation of the BEF from Dunkirk. He had served as an escort on five occasions, although this was the first time he had done so with Lance Corporal Dunlop; he had never received any orders about firing his weapon. He then described how the local police had told the escort that it would be better to leave Private Fitzgerald in the cells and then take a police car to the station.

Under cross-examination Private Sheppard admitted that if he had been in charge of the escort he would not have taken the prisoner into public houses. Sheppard then described how in one public house in Lochee the prisoner had gone outside to talk to his wife and he had overheard someone say 'there's a move on'. Becoming suspicious he went outside and found the prisoner and his wife in the company of a police constable. He had asked Fitzgerald if he was all right and the prisoner had then followed him back into the pub. Sheppard told the court that he believed this may have been an abortive escape attempt.

He then explained how Fitzgerald was a very plausible and persuasive man but that he suspected that he was trying to gull his guards into missing the train. Sheppard then went on to describe another incident in a public house near the station. While the guards were talking to some civilians Fitzgerald left the pub. Sheppard followed him out of the pub and saw him 20 yards up the street in the opposite direction to the station. He immediately ordered him to halt and loaded his rifle, with the safety catch on. When Fitzgerald saw him load his rifle he stopped and was taken back into custody. In his opinion this was a definite escape attempt and the prisoner had only given in when he had become convinced that Sheppard was taking his duty seriously and would fire.

Sheppard also testified that in his opinion the dead man was pretending to be drunk. He had served with him in France and had seen him drink a lot more than he had on that occasion. After his recapture, Lance Corporal Dunlop had come up to him and said to the prisoner 'You are finished now. We'll go to the station', telling the prisoner to 'play the game', before saying to Private Sheppard, 'Don't stand any more nonsense from him. Fire.'[4]

Shepherd then testified as to the events that led up to the shooting. When the lance corporal had left him, he had told the prisoner to 'play the game' as the NCO had with him all day and they had shaken hands. Almost immediately, however, he deliberately began to walk away. Sheppard had ordered the prisoner to halt or he would fire and had placed the rifle to his shoulder when the prisoner refused to stop. On seeing him raise his rifle he described how Fitzgerald had half-turned and waved his hand. Private Sheppard believed that his intention was to get onto the street where, with the guards being strangers to Dundee, he could have lost them.

Under cross-examination Sheppard said that he believed he was carrying out his duty correctly, that he had intended to fire into the wooden partition behind the prisoner as a warning, but the movement of Fitzgerald meant that the bullet struck him. He had no intention of killing or even wounding him. He also stated that the previous five weeks had taken their toll on him and that there was no-one who was more sorry at what had happened. He agreed that it was very unusual to take a prisoner to see his family, to have drinks and to attend a football match but said that he was acting under the orders of the lance lorporal as a soldier should.

The prosecution alleged that all three men had been under the influence of drink and that the accused had not been himself on that night and had fired without thinking. Private Sheppard firmly denied this and reiterated that he knew, after the police had failed, that he would not be able to persuade the lance corporal to leave Fitzgerald in the cells. Furthermore, it would be a very serious matter for a private to disobey the orders of a superior unless he was absolutely sure that the superior was drunk and incapable.

The jury was instructed that the prosecution case rested entirely on the fact that the conduct of the accused on the night in question was without justification and utterly reckless and that the orders given to him by his NCO were so unreasonable that a soldier should not have obeyed them. The defence addressed the jury, telling them that the reduction in charge made no difference to the accused as he intended to gain a full acquittal. There had been a killing, but the fact that there had been no criminal intent or recklessness meant that there was no crime. Furthermore, it was paramount that soldiers be encouraged to obey orders and perform their duties. He completed his address by saying that, although Sheppard had consumed some beer, he was quite capable of performing his duty in a responsible manner.

In his summing up, Lord Robertson stated the seriousness of the case before reminding the jury that the accused was a soldier escorting a deserter and it seemed to him that a guilty charge might result in soldiers on duty being paralysed to the detriment of national interests. The jury returned after just five minutes and gave a unanimous verdict of not guilty. After Private Sheppard had stepped down from the dock he shook hands with his counsel and received congratulations from several soldiers from his unit.

Some few of the evacuees from Dundee undoubtedly had only themselves to blame for the trouble that they encountered. At the beginning of July an unnamed 9-year-old Dundee evacuee found himself charged at Perth Juvenile Court with having thrown a stone at a railway engine causing injury to the driver. At 6:40pm on 19 June the boy had been standing on a bridge when a train from Alyth Junction to Alyth passed beneath. He had thrown a stone at the engine and broke some glass with splinters hitting the driver and injuring his hands. Sheriff Valentine put the boy on probation for a year.

Although the public were expected to look up to the men serving in uniform, not all of them were admirable. On 4 July two brothers who were serving soldiers found themselves before the Sheriff charged with several counts of theft. The ringleader was the elder brother, Private John Stewart (20) of the Cameronians. This was the same young man who had been sent to prison for two months in 1940. John had three previous convictions for theft and his punishments had included a term at an approved school. He and his younger brother, Private William Stewart (19) of the Black Watch, had pleaded guilty to three counts of theft from three separate Dundee houses. The first robbery was at 80 Blackness Road, occupied by Christina Stewart, the men's aunt, when a pair of trousers had been stolen. The second occurred at 143 Nethergate, occupied by Achhar Sidhu, when a suit had been stolen, and the third theft had happened at 1 Peter Street, occupied by Jessie Lindsay, when Private John Stewart, acting alone, had stolen a pair of curtains.

The procurator-fiscal, Mr D.J. Henry, stated that it was unfortunate that the two men had been granted leave together as the elder brother had clearly influenced his younger sibling to aid in the crimes. He also stated that the elder brother had told the police that he was trying to get into civvies (civilian clothing) and it seems likely that he was perhaps planning to desert. In sentencing Private John Stewart, Sheriff Malcolm branded him 'an incorrigible thief' and gave him two months' imprisonment. The younger brother was admonished and warned as to his future conduct.

August saw the transfer of 751 Naval Air Squadron from Arbroath to HMS *Condor II* at Dundee. The squadron was equipped with the Supermarine Walrus and was engaged in air-sea rescue and maritime reconnaissance. During its time at Dundee it undertook such duties and combined this with offering important catapult training for Walrus crews.

The people of Dundee were treated to a rare sight on 5 August when three British tanks swept through the city as part of the Speed the Tanks campaign. When the armoured vehicles parked up in Bell Street they were mobbed by a crowd of over 100 adults and children who clambered all over them. The tanks were led by a small scout car called a Bren Carrier which carried a driver and gunner armed with a Bren machine-gun. The small, lightly armoured, vehicle was capable of speeds of up to 50 mph and was used for scouting ahead of armoured formations. The main attraction, however, was the Matilda tank named 'Auld Reekie'. The Matilda weighed in at around 27 tons and was armed with a 2-pounder (40mm) gun in a three-man turret and a Besa machine-gun. It carried a crew of four and the type had seen extensive action in France and North Africa. Accompanying the Matilda were two Cruiser VI, tanks. These lighter, faster, tanks had also seen extensive action in North Africa. At first it was men who were most interested in the tanks but 70-year-old Mrs Scott of 31 Liff Road, Lochee, joined them in climbing onto the tanks. Mrs Scott told reporters that she had a double interest in that both her father and her husband had been soldiers.

Shortly after the tanks had arrived at City Square, the acting-Provost, Bailie Burgoyne, welcomed Lieutenant Hallis and his men to the city while the city's salvage officer, Mr W.H. Sagar, took the opportunity to ask the people of Dundee to put every effort into the salvage drive which was to begin shortly. He told them that if Britain was to have more tanks such as these then the donation of scrap metal was vital. He was sure that the people of Dundee would donate tons of railings which were useless around their houses, but which would be invaluable to the war effort if they were turned into tanks and other weapons. Typically, the spirit of competitiveness played a part and Mr Sagar added that he believed that the people of Dundee would not wish to be seen as less patriotic than the people of Edinburgh, who had already donated 460 tons of railings.

A three-year-old Dundee boy was the victim of a tragic accident on 21 October when a lorry came off the road and crashed into his parents' house at Bogmill, Inchture. Douglas McLean was playing in

Tanks on display in Dundee. The Matilda is in the foreground with a Crusader in the background. (Dundee Evening Telegraph)

the garden when the lorry crashed through the wooden fence and hit him. The lorry, which belonged to a Glasgow firm, was travelling from Inchture to Errol when it left the road. Douglas was the only child of Mr and Mrs McLean. The family lived at 21 Morgan Street, Dundee but Douglas had been living with his mother in the family's country home at Bogmill since the beginning of the war. His father, Robert, was serving in England with the Royal Corps of Signals.

The children who were sent to Belmont Camp near Cupar Angus were often from rougher and poorer areas and there were problems with some of the boys repeatedly running away. The fact that Dundee was so close was a constant draw to them. Some of the parents had also been problematic and had been visiting outside of the appointed days and this had fostered discontent. The authorities attempted to remedy the situation by recruiting boys 'of the right type from primary schools, but some were withdrawn because the company was "too rough"'.[5] Many of the boys at the camp did not take kindly to the discipline and regulation with many resenting the routines of bathing and washing, the regular meal hours or the early lights out. The diet, which was said by the authorities to be admirable, also came in for criticism with many boys being more used to a diet of chips and occasional 'pieces' with tea. It was thought by the authorities that sending boys in class groups and for limited periods of a month or six weeks might popularise the camp and be seen as more of a country holiday.

A large number of Dundee children were experiencing a 'holiday' of a different kind and were employed in lifting potatoes in the area of Carnoustie. Although the majority of children enjoyed this experience there were some problems. Some of those involved in the scheme complained in mid-October that one group had not been fed on one occasion and had received only soup and half a pie each on another occasion. It appears that this was a result of a mistake on the part of the authorities as the kitchen staff had prepared an excellent meal for the children but had been informed that as the weather was wet they would not be at the farm. Bailie Webster argued that some children not registered on the scheme had been gate-crashing and this was adding to the confusion and muddle. The committee agreed with him and decided to form a sub-committee to inquire into the workings of the scheme and to decide if the appointment of a deputy director of education might be required to oversee the scheme.

A Dundee-built merchant ship the SS *Tantalus* found some measure of fame due to the heroic efforts of her crew. Built at Caledon, she had been transferred to the Glen Line in 1936 and briefly renamed the SS *Radnorshire* before reverting to her original name in 1939. By 1941 she was awaiting a refit in Hong Kong when the Japanese invaded. With the Japanese troops on the outskirts of the city her crew bravely managed to get her underway and made for Manila. Arriving during an air raid, it was decided to make for Bataan instead (under tow) but she was hit by bombs, set on fire and capsized in Manila Bay. Her courageous crew were captured by the Japanese forces and several of them did not survive the experience as PoWs, with at least two being executed after unsuccessful escape attempts.

The SS *Gorgon*, another Caledon ship, launched in 1933, also found fame when she successfully evacuated 359 refugees from Singapore just days before the fall of the colony. The *Gorgon* and her crew managed this feat despite being heavily bombed by Japanese aircraft throughout the operation. The crew later discovered an unexploded bomb in a stack of flour in the hold which they brought up onto the deck and casually rolled overboard. The *Gorgon* survived the war to be scrapped in 1964.

On 2 November a lone German raider flew over the Dundee area and dropped four bombs. One fell in a field at Linlathen, another at Blairfield Farm and two fell at Mains of Wellbank. Damage was very slight and there were no injuries.

1942

Flying in the crowded skies of wartime Britain was never without risk and many airmen lost their lives due to collisions. On the afternoon of 17 January 1942, however, a Dundee airman and his crew were lost in circumstances which could easily have been avoided. Stirling I (W7467) of 7 Squadron had taken off on a training flight but at approximately 3:40pm a trainee Hurricane pilot from 56 OTU decided to make an unauthorised practice attack on the bomber despite the hazy conditions. The trainee fighter pilot misjudged his attack and collided with the Stirling causing both aircraft to crash near Cambridge. There were eight men in the Stirling and all were killed including the flight engineer Sergeant Edward Blacklaw, a 21-year-old Dundonian.[6]

The war in the air was often seen as being dominated by Bomber and Fighter Command with Coastal Command not attracting quite the same attention, but Coastal Command undertook many vital duties. One of the most dangerous and important of these was the interdiction of enemy shipping. One of the squadrons involved in these missions was 217 Squadron based at St Eval, with a detachment at Thorney Island, which was equipped with the Bristol Beaufort. On 12 February Beaufort II (AW278, F) was lost when attacking enemy shipping off the

Dutch coast. One of the crew was Sergeant David Yule Fyfe (27), the son of Charles and Helen Fyfe of Dundee.[7]

The enforcement of blackout regulations continued to be harsh and the authorities had stepped up punishments as it seemed that a large number of the residents of Dundee and the surrounding areas had become rather complacent due to the lack of raiding. On 11 March Honorary Sheriff-Substitute C.H. Marshall heard the cases of sixty-seven offenders. He let one offender off with an admonishment, but the remaining sixty-six were fined sums raging from 10s to £1.

Early March also saw the death of yet another local airman when Sergeant Crichton Alexander Smith died from injuries sustained while flying with 61 OTU. Sergeant Smith (21) was the eldest son of Mr and Mrs George Smith of 'Dyalla', Balmoral Road, Blairgowrie. Educated at Blairgowrie High School, he had worked at the Blairgowrie branch of the Union Bank before volunteering for RAF service in December 1940. Sergeant Smith was a keen sportsman taking part in cricket, golf, football and swimming as well as angling. His parents brought their son's body back home for burial at Blairgowrie Cemetery.

Just six days after the death of Sergeant Smith another Dundee airman lost his life. The 9 Squadron crew of Sergeant J. Doughty had taken off from RAF Honington at 12:31am on the morning of 9 March and was last detected as being off-track over the North Sea at 1:27am. Nothing further was heard from the crew and the aircraft was posted missing. David and Elizabeth Stirling received news at their Dundee home that their son, Sergeant Ewen Ritchie Stirling, the wireless operator/air gunner in the crew, had failed to return from operations and had been posted missing believed killed. Nothing more was ever seen or heard of the six-man crew of Wellington III (X3641) and all are commemorated on the Runnymede Memorial.

We have already seen how the authorities in Dundee were exhorting people to give up their metal railings for the war effort being told that scrap metals would be used to build aircraft, tanks and other much-needed weapons. The campaign continued into 1942 with donations continuing to be made. The corporation set an example and the railings surrounding many of their properties were removed for the scheme and in March the iron railings which surrounded the burial ground at Constitution Road were sacrificed.

At the start of April a major fire broke out at one of Dundee's jute manufacturers. When the fire brigade arrived, flames were shooting from the door of the Seafield Works of Thomson, Shepherd & Co. Ltd., on Taylor's Lane. The fire was confined to the north end of the building in an area which was used as a store and began when a bale of jute fell onto and broke a cable that was being used to power an electric winch. There were some 6,800 bales of jute in the store and the fire was completely out of control when the fire brigade arrived. It swept through the building. The area around the factory was extremely tight and firemen were forced to scale nearby roofs on Taylor's Lane, Perth Road and Shepherd's Lane in order to pour water onto the blaze.

Collecting railings in Constitution Road. (Dundee Evening Telegraph)

Firemen deployed approximately half a mile of hoses, which had to be dragged through tenement closes and back-greens to pour tons of water onto the blaze. When the roof collapsed dense clouds of smoke billowed up and blackened the windows of nearby tenements. The fire brigade remained at the scene overnight and one of the factory walls collapsed into a back-green during the night. The damage to the factory was put at between £45,000–£50,000.

Throughout the year the Dundee men who were flying as part of Bomber Command's offensive against Germany continued to pay the supreme price. On the night of 1/2 April the command sent a force of forty-nine aircraft to make an experimental low-level attack on railway targets at Hanau and Lohr. Only twenty-two aircraft reported attacking the targets successfully and losses were unsustainably high with thirteen aircraft lost. Twelve of these were Wellingtons and this represented over 34 per cent of the Wellington force on this raid. One squadron, No.57, lost five aircraft, while 214 Squadron lost four. Wellington IC (Z8805) was lost without trace with the crew of Sergeant E. Dixon. The wireless operator/air gunner in the Wellington

Dundee jute factory fire at the Seafield Works. (Dundee Evening Telegraph)

was Pilot Officer James McKenzie Henderson, a 26-year-old married man from Dundee.[8]

On the night of 2/3 June the target for Bomber Command was Essen; 195 aircraft were sent on the raid but the haze which hung over this target once again meant that bombing was badly scattered. The records in Essen recorded only three high explosive bombs and 300 incendiaries. For this meagre return the command lost fourteen aircraft. Amongst them was the 15 Squadron crew of Warrant Officer A.J. Cowirick, RNZAF. Stirling I (N3728, LS-T) was shot down by a night fighter over Holland with the deaths of all seven of the crew. The bomb aimer in the crew was Dundonian Sergeant Frederick Gordon Crighton (21). His parents, Andrew and Jemima Crighton, received the news that their only son had failed to return from operations and had been posted missing at their home at 16 Corso Street. Sergeant Crighton, who had joined the RAF in 1941, had been educated at Logie Central School. He was a member of the Dundee Cycle Club and Chalmers Church Boys' Brigade and had been a photographer with Valentine & Sons Ltd. In January 1943 his parents received the news that their son was now presumed to have been killed. Sergeant Crighton was buried at Jonkerbos War Cemetery, Nijmegen where his parents and sisters had the following inscription placed upon his headstone: LOVING MEMORIES OF OUR DEAR SON AND BROTHER. MUM, DAD, ELLA AND MOIRA.

The memory of the many Dundee airmen who lost their lives has not been forgotten and an article in the *Dundee Courier* of 13 February 1996 explained how a group (the *Histoire et Collection – Douarnenez 39-45*) in France, had been formed with the aim of preserving the memory of wartime events on the western tip of the Brittany peninsula. The group was looking for information on three Dundee airmen who were buried locally. Sergeant Gerard Joseph Laing, the son of William and Teresa Laing, who was a 21-year-old wireless operator/air gunner, killed on the same night as Sergeant Crighton, while serving with 420 (Snowy Owl) (RCAF) Squadron. His crew, under the command of Sergeant E. Harrison, was lost in Hampden I (AE260, PT-O) on a 'gardening' (minelaying) operation off Lorient.[9] It was not until January 1943 that it was confirmed that Sergeant Laing had been killed. He had been educated at St John's Central School in Dundee, Blackrock College, Dublin and Castlehead College, England, before he joined the RAF in 1940. He had four older brothers who were also serving (two in the Army and two in the RAF).

The collection and salvaging of wastepaper attracted a great deal of attention throughout the war and the spring of 1942 saw a keen sense of competition between the local schools in Dundee. The cleansing superintendent, Mr W.H. Sagar, had been one of those who was keen to increase the tonnage collected by encouraging this sense of friendly competition and prizes were awarded for schools which had collected the most waste paper. In the first week of September it was announced that the winners were Downfield School. The first prize for this feat was the award of a new cine camera. The headmaster, Mr Charles Mowatt, accepted the prize awarded by Lord Provost Wilson. He was accompanied by the regional controller of the Waste Paper Recovery Association, Mr C.A. Anderson, the

Sgt Gerard Joseph Laing, RAF.
(Dundee Courier)

Sgt Frederick Gordon Crighton, RAF.
(Dundee Courier)

convenor of the Dundee Education Committee, ex-Bailie Robert Loggie, the director of education, Mr John R. Cameron and Mr Sagar.

By this stage of the war the manpower shortages in many industries were reaching a critical stage and the earlier reluctance of some companies to employ women in roles which, until then, had been the preserve of men was weakening due to necessity. In early June the LMS was training several women to take on the role of guards. The earlier feelings towards the employment of married women were also changing and several of these trainee guards were married.

On the night of 25/26 June Bomber Harris launched the third of his thousand bomber raids (although only 960 aircraft took part). To assemble such a force Bomber Command had to rely on many aircraft

Mrs Middleton, one of a number of trainee guards for the LMS synchronises her watch with the duty train driver. (Dundee Evening Telegraph)

The presentation at Downfield School. (Dundee Evening Telegraph)

and crews being supplied from the training units and on this occasion the aircraft from the OTUs suffered heavy losses. No.24 OTU sent a number of Whitleys and lost three. Amongst them was Whitley V (BD379) piloted by Flying Officer J.B. Munro, RNZAF. The bomber took off from RAF Honeybourne at 10:20pm but shortly after 4am was heard transmitting an SOS. Nothing further was heard but the German authorities later reported that bodies of four of the five crew had washed ashore. The wireless operator in the crew was Pilot Officer Ian Patterson Clark (27) from Dundee.[10]

The attitude towards the Home Guard continued to change as the force took on new and more varied duties. Some Home Guards were already manning anti-aircraft and searchlight batteries, while others were providing guards for coastal batteries and some were even trained to man these batteries. By June the Home Forces of the regular Army were increasingly anxious to free up additional manpower and ordered the closure of some batteries in Scotland while at others the

Home Guard was ordered to man the coastal defence batteries. The Stannergate Battery, for example, was manned by men drawn from the 1st and 2nd City of Dundee Battalions of the Home Guard. By the following month there were twenty fully trained, eighteen partly trained and thirty-five new recruits from the Home Guard manning the Stannergate Battery. Four weeks later the battery was fully manned by three officers and eighty other ranks from the Dundee Home Guard.

For the men of Bomber Command their training was often nearly as dangerous as the operations. On 19 August Lancaster I (R5863) of 207 Squadron crashed at 1:15am at Normanton in Nottinghamshire while its crew were practising overshoot procedure on three engines. The crew of six were all killed instantly. Amongst them was Pilot Officer Denis Victor Morris-Edwards, a 20-year-old airman who was married to Corinne Mae Morris-Edwards of Dundee.[11]

The actions of the Merchant Navy were increasingly vital throughout the war, but the losses suffered by the men of the service were very severe. By 1942 the Merchant Navy was also mounting incredibly dangerous convoys to Russia to provide supplies to that nation. Conditions and losses on this route were heavy as the Germans knew that these supplies were vital to Russia. The MV *Atheltemplar* was a motor tanker which before the war had been run by the United Molasses Company and Athel Lines. By September the tanker had completed at least nineteen crossings of the Atlantic and was now operating on the Arctic convoys to Russia. Earlier in the year the ship had been damaged. She was repaired at North Shields and left the Tyne to join Convoy PQ18. The previous convoy had sustained very heavy losses and this was to be no different. The convoy was spotted by Luftwaffe patrols and, despite the efforts of Sea Hurricanes from the escort carrier HMS *Avenger* in chasing away a Blohm & Voss BV138 *Seedrache* seaplane, managed to vector in U-boats.

On 13 September the convoy came under sustained attack by U-boats and from the air. During the day a gunner on the *Atheltemplar* shot down a Junkers Ju88, but in the early hours of 14 September the tanker was hit by a torpedo fired by *U-457*. The tanker caught fire and the master ordered the crew to abandon ship. The *Atheltemplar* had a crew complement of sixty-one and all but three were saved. Amongst the dead was Senior 4th Engineer John Todd Wilson, aged 22, a former Morgan Academy pupil. He had served his apprenticeship as an engineer with the Caledon Yard and joined the Merchant Navy in 1940. He came from a maritime tradition as his grandfather, Captain John Todd, had worked for the Tay Steamboat Company. The news of the loss of their eldest son was delivered to Mr and Mrs V.C. Wilson at 21 Fairfield Road.[12]

The day before the *Atheltemplar* was sunk the Halcyon-class minesweeper HMS *Leda* had set out from Russia as part of the escort for Convoy QP14 which was

Right: *Senior 4th Engineer John Todd Wilson.* (Dundee Courier)

Below: *MC* Atheltemplar. (Public Domain)

A Blohm & Voss BV138 Seedrache *seaplane of the type driven off by Sea Hurricanes.* (Public Domain)

returning to Greenland. During the journey the minesweeper reported that her sonar had broken down and at 5:30am on 20 September she was hit by two torpedoes fired from *U-435*. The minesweeper took over an hour to sink in the icy waters of the Greenland Sea south of Spitsbergen. The captain, eighty-six of his crew and two Merchant Navy officers were rescued from the minesweeper but forty-three members of the crew lost their lives. Amongst them was Leading Steward Alexander Christison, the 21-year-old son of Mr and Mrs Norman Christison. Leading Steward Christison was from the rural hamlet of Redford, Carmyllie and had joined the Royal Navy when he was aged just 18. One of his brothers was a PoW and he had another who was serving in Gibraltar.[13]

Wing Commander Hugh Gordon Malcolm (25) had taken over command of 18 Squadron in Tunisia late in the year and the Broughty Ferry airman quickly demonstrated his courage. This was particularly the case on 17 November when he led an attack on Bizerta. The Bristol Blenheims took advantage of low cloud cover but when they were still 20 miles from the target the sky cleared. Knowing the danger they were in with no fighter escort, Wing Commander Malcolm could well have chosen to abort the operation but instead he pressed on to

Right: *Leading Steward Alexander Christison.* (Public Domain)

Below: *HMS* Leda. (Public Domain)

the target. Despite fierce opposition the attack was a success with the airfield bombed and several aircraft knocked out on the ground, while the Blenheims also shot down an Me109 fighter and a Ju52 transport aircraft.

On 4 December Wing Commander Hugh Malcolm was tasked with leading an attack by thirteen Bristol Blenheims from his own 18 Squadron and 614 Squadron. Only nine of the aircraft managed

Wing Commander Hugh Gordon Malcolm VC, MiD. (Public Domain)

to find the target which was Robb aerodrome in Tunisia. As the British aircraft began their attack they were intercepted by a large force of enemy fighters and one by one they were all shot down. Wing Commander Malcolm and his crew were in Blenheim V (BA875, W) which was the final bomber to be lost, shot down in flames 20km from Chouigui. For his courage on this operation and on operations on 17 and 28 November, Wing Commander Malcolm was awarded the Victoria Cross.[14] Born in Broughty Ferry, Wing Commander Malcolm had entered RAF College Cranwell in January 1936. In May 1939 he was injured in a crash involving a Westland Lysander. After recovering from his injuries he served in a training role before serving as Air Liaison Officer to Lieutenant General Bernard Montgomery.

CHAPTER 4

1943–1944 – The Turn of the Tide

The wartime atmosphere led to an increase in the number of weddings with many being between young men and women who were both serving in uniform, including some of different nationalities. One such wedding took place at Dundee City's Register Office on 11 January when Leading Aircraftwoman Kathleen Wallace, WAAF, and Sapper W.H. Warnock of the New Zealand Forestry Corps tied the knot. Even the witnesses were in uniform, Mrs Townsend in that of the WRNS and Sapper P.V. Wastney in that of both his and the groom's corps.

With the risk of invasion now gone the Home Guard was increasingly used in other duties but still expected to be a part of any defence against any airborne or raiding parties. The regular Army commander in the area developed a plan consisting of a series of observation posts, manned roadblocks and defensive positions in the city itself. The new plan developed into a scheme in which the Home Guard would defend strategic points such as Balgay Hill and Dundee Law in addition to several key buildings within the city.

On the night of 15/16 January Bomber Command launched its second attack in two nights on Lorient. The raid was accurate with at least 800 buildings destroyed. There were also several minor operations including two Mosquitoes testing Oboe (a radar bombing aid) in a raid on Aachen and nine Wellingtons laying mines off Lorient and St Nazaire. Bomber Command was also responsible for the maintenance and staffing of several squadrons which flew covert operations to supply and support resistance movements through the auspices of the Special Operations Executive (SOE). Amongst these was 161 Squadron which had been formed from the King's Flight and elements of 138 Squadron. The squadron had recently re-equipped with the Halifax V bomber and, on this night, it suffered its first loss. Halifax V (DG285, MA-X) had taken off from RAF Tempsford in Bedfordshire but nothing further was heard and later reports confirmed that the Halifax crashed near Rennes, killing all seven of the crew. The navigator or flight engineer (accounts differ) in the crew was a Dundee man. Sergeant Stewart McKenzie Anderson, the 21-year-old son of Hugh and Isabella Anderson, was buried with the rest of the crew at Rennes Eastern Communal Cemetery. Sergeant Anderson was one of those three airmen that the *Histoire et Collection – Douarnenez 39-45* group were researching in 1996.

On the following night the men of Bomber Command were sent to mount an attack on Berlin with 201 aircraft (mainly Lancasters). This was the first time an all four-engine force had been dispatched and was also the first time that target indicators were used to mark the aiming point. The raid was, however, a disappointment with poor bombing results, although only one aircraft was lost. The next night the attempt was repeated with similar results in terms of bombing, but the use of the same route on the long haul to the German capital enabled the German night fighters to locate the bomber stream with the result that twenty-two aircraft were lost. It was a particularly bleak night for 12 Squadron at RAF Wickenby which lost four aircraft. Amongst them was Lancaster I (W4372, PH-G) under the command of Sergeant E.B. Withell, RNZAF. The bomber was lost at some point over the North Sea. Of the seven-man crew only one body was recovered. This was Sergeant Andrew Mitchell, the 33-year-old mid-upper air gunner, the son of Andrew and Agnes Mitchell of Dundee and the husband of Phyllis Comrie Mitchell. Sergeant Mitchell's body was recovered from the sea and he lies in Esbjerg (Fourfelt) Cemetery. His six comrades are commemorated on the Runnymede Memorial.[1]

Bomber Command's campaign against the U-boat bases near the Bay of Biscay continued throughout the early months of the war and on the night of 7/8 February yet another attack was made against Lorient.

This was a major raid involving 323 aircraft and proved to be a devastating attack for the loss of seven aircraft. At least two Dundee airmen were killed on this operation. Sergeant William Harris Cowman was a 22-year-old wireless operator in the 408 (Goose) (RCAF) Squadron crew of Flight Sergeant D.W. Smith, RCAF. The crew had taken off from RAF Leeming in Halifax II (HR655, EQ-S) at 7:08pm but nothing further was heard and they were posted missing. Later reports confirmed that the Halifax had crashed over France and all seven of the crew were buried in Guidel Communal Cemetery.

The second Dundonian fatality of the raid was Sergeant David Coventry Pennycook, a 21-year-old bomb aimer with 199 Squadron. The crew of Flight Lieutenant K. Powell had taken off in Wellington III (BK507, EX-E) from RAF Ingham, but the aircraft crashed in the target area with the loss of all six men aboard. Like Sergeant Cowman and his crew, the crew of Sergeant Pennycook are buried in Guidel Communal Cemetery. Sergeant Pennycook was the third airman of whom information was being sought by the *Histoire et Collection – Douarnenez 39-45* group in the 1990s.

Not all of the RAF losses during February were made up of members of Bomber Command. On 14 February Bristol Beaufighter VI (JL647) of 301 Ferry Training Unit (FTU) was being ferried from Gibraltar to Bilda, Algeria, but failed to arrive. It appears likely that the Beaufighter went down over the Mediterranean, killing both crew, one of which was Sergeant George Robb Watson Ross, son of David and Lizzie Ross from Lochee.[2]

In March the escort carrier HMS *Dasher* arrived on the Tay for repair at the Caledon Yard. She had been badly damaged during an Arctic convoy but was needed urgently for her duties. HMS *Dasher* was one of the Avenger-class escort carriers which were American built, converted from type C3 merchant vessels and based on the US Navy's Long Island-class of carrier. The yard repaired the damage and extended her flight deck in just four days and the carrier sailed for the Clyde. This was despite the fact that an electrical fault had started a fire at one point when she was being repaired. HMS *Dasher* participated in the escort of one convoy but, setting out to escort a second, she suffered engine problems and turned back.

On 27 March she was on the Clyde when she suffered a catastrophic internal explosion which sent her to the bottom in just minutes. The blame for the disaster, which resulted in the loss of 379 men from her 528-man crew, was hushed up by the authorities and many of the casualties were buried in an unknown mass grave at either Ardrossan or Greenock. This caused great distress and anger amongst the relatives of the dead. There were various theories surrounding the loss of HMS *Dasher* with the most likely being that the explosion had occurred because of the poor design of the stowage and handling facilities of the ship's fuel. Certainly, the stowage of fuel on her British sister ships was subsequently reduced by more than 50 per cent and the US Navy also reduced their stowage figures. Others put forward the claim that one of the carrier's Fairey Swordfish aircraft had crashed into HMS *Dasher* and set off a chain of explosions. The US authorities at first tried to put the blame on poor petrol handling procedures in the Royal Navy. Whatever the cause, the loss was covered up, most likely to maintain morale and to avoid any speculation over faulty US construction.[3]

The Caledon Yard had a number of merchant contracts on its books when the war began. One of these was for a refrigerated cargo vessel named the MV *Telemachus* for the Alfred Holt Line. In 1941, however, the Ministry of War Transport took over the contract and she was destined to become the MV *Empire Activity*. However, at the beginning of 1942 the contract was once again taken over, this time by the Admiralty, and she was redesigned as an escort carrier named HMS *Activity*. Launched at the end of May and commissioned in September, she went on to provide useful service escorting convoys in the Atlantic and the Arctic before acting as a ferry carrier taking personnel and equipment to the Far East. HMS *Activity* was then sent to Singapore to support the re-occupation and ended her wartime service by bringing former PoWs and other passengers home to Britain.[4]

HMS Dasher. (Public Domain)

HMS Activity. (Public Domain)

The Caledon Yard remained busy throughout the year with work on both merchant vessels, submarines and on three Castle-class corvettes. HMS *Carisbrooke Castle* was laid down in March, launched at the end of July and commissioned in November. HMS *Dumbarton Castle* was laid down in May, launched in September and commissioned in February 1944. HMS *Hurst Castle* was laid down in August, launched in late February but was not commissioned until June 1944.

On the night of 5/6 March RAF Bomber Command launched the first stage of its Main Offensive with what became known as the Battle of the Ruhr. The battle opened with a raid on Essen but 'Bomber' Harris, the commander of Bomber Command, realised he could not solely attack targets in the Ruhr and on the night of 8/9 March he sent a force of 335 aircraft to attack Nuremburg in the south of Germany. One of the eight aircraft which failed to return from the operation was that of Flight Lieutenant C.A. Giles, DFC, RAAF, of 61 Squadron based at RAF Syerston. The rear gunner in the crew was 21-year-old Flight Sergeant Douglas Forbes from Dundee. His Lancaster I (W4903, QR-P) is believed to have crashed in the vicinity of Furth and all the crew are buried in Durnbach War Cemetery.

At the end of March Bomber Command once again attempted to mount an attack on the German capital when 329 aircraft were dispatched in what turned out to be very poor weather conditions, with icing at altitude and inaccurately forecast winds. As a result, most of the bombs fell in open countryside. All of this came for the loss of twenty-one aircraft. At RAF Lissett 158 Squadron lost just one aircraft, Halifax II (HR757, NP-M) with Warrant Officer H. Holcombe and his crew. The Halifax was hit by flak and crashed in the suburbs of Hamburg. The rear gunner in the crew was Sergeant Ernest Milne, a 22-year-old Dundonian.[5]

Throughout the year the day bomber squadrons on 2 Group, Bomber Command, carried out a variety of raids against targets in Occupied Europe and against enemy shipping and port facilities. Many of these operations proved costly as enemy fighter and flak opposition was deadly. On 5 April twelve Lockheed Venturas of 21 Squadron were sent to bomb a tanker lying at Brest. The ship was not hit, although nearby dock facilities were, but flak and fighter opposition was heavy and four of the Venturas failed to return. Sergeant Eric James Andrew (28) from Dundee, was the pilot of Ventura II (AE852, YH-S). Sergeant Andrew's aircraft was last seen being chased out to sea by Focke Wulf Fw190 fighters and was shot down some 30km off the coast, killing all four crew.[6] Sergeant Andrew's loss was announced while the Dundee Wings for Victory campaign was ongoing and provided a further spur to support the campaign in his community of Barnhill, Broughty Ferry.

By the spring the Axis forces in North Africa were in full retreat having moved along the Libyan coast into Tunisia. Successive defensive lines had, however, been set up and the assaults on the Axis positions at Medenine, the Mareth Line and Wadi Akarit in March and April, while successful, were costly. Amongst the Dundee men to lose their lives in this period was Private George Keir. The 20-year-old soldier was serving with the 7th Black Watch when he was killed on 6 April. Private Keir was the only son of George and Betsy Keir of 35 Lawrence Street. He had been educated at Logie Central School and had been a member of the 4th (St Mark's) Boys' Brigade Company. Before enlisting he had been an apprentice moulder at Lawside Foundry.[7]

On 11 April another young Dundonian pilot lost his life on operations with Bomber Command. On the night of 10/11 April the command sent 502 aircraft to Frankfurt on a raid which was, once again, thwarted by cloud cover

Sgt E.J. Andrew. (Broughty Ferry Guide)

Privt George Keir. (Dundee Evening Telegraph)

over the target. Among the twenty-one aircraft which failed to return were two from 75 (New Zealand) Squadron. Stirling III (BF456, AA-J) was shot down and crashed at Steeg. The pilot was Sergeant John Webb (23), son of John and Isabella M. Webb of Dundee.[8] The inscription on his grave reads: UNTIL THE DAY BREAK, AND THE SHADOWS FLEE AWAY.

Dundee's Wings for Victory campaign was to take place between 24 April and 1 May and a wide variety of events were planned as part of the campaign. A number of communities organised dances to raise funds for the cause. Typical of these was that organised by Mrs C.M. Chalmers of 2 Park Place, Ancrum Road, which took place in the Albert Hall in Lochee. A number of artistes were booked to take part, while musical accompaniment was provided by the band of 1232 Squadron Air Training Corps (ATC). The dance was a success and raised the sum of £18 for the Wings for Victory campaign.

This campaign started on Saturday 24 April and it was announced that one of the main attractions was to be the display of two aircraft in City Square. The aircraft were a Hawker Hurricane of the RAF and a Grumman Martlet (the Grumman F4F Wildcat, renamed for British service) of the Fleet Air Arm. A very ambitious target of £3,000,000 had been set and it was said that it would be used to purchase 200 fighters and 50 heavy bombers. The campaign was to be officially opened at 11am, when the Provost was to speak from the daylight cinema van in the City Square. He was to be accompanied by Group Captain G.C. Pinkerton DFC. Pinkerton was the first man to be credited with the shooting down of a German bomber over Britain during the

Dundee Wings for Victory Campaign advert. (Broughty Ferry Guide)

Grumman F4F Martlet of the Fleet Air Arm. (Public Domain)

war. The parade to mark the beginning of the campaign began at 3pm and included 2,000 representatives from the services, Home Guard and civil defence and was to start at Riverside Drive before proceeding down South Union Street, Dock Street, Trades Lane, St Andrews Street, Cowgate and Murraygate before the salute was taken by Provost Wilson

at the stand in City Square. A first for a Dundee wartime parade would be the presence of a squadron of Australian airmen.

The campaign got off to a very promising start and by the end of the first day a total of £1,723,141 had been raised. This was £80,000 more than had been achieved on the first day of the Warships Week campaign

Lord Provost Garnet Wilson, in the uniform of the Lord Lieutenant, takes the salute at the Wings for Victory parade. (Broughty Ferry Guide)

and represented more than half of the total which was being aimed at. As a result, it was hoped that the eventual total might eventually top £4,000,000.

The people of Dundee were bombarded with adverts for the campaign, many of which exhorted them to support the RAF as it had been the RAF which had sustained and fortified the nation during its darkest hour, and it was now taking the war to Germany in ever greater strength. The aim of raising £3,000,000 was an ambitious one but it was hoped by the organisers that the Warship Week total of £3,711,712 might be exceeded. This was interesting as the key role which people were aware of involving the RAF at the time was the bombing of Germany by the heavy bombers of RAF Bomber Command. The images of Spitfires, however, were powerful when it came to inspiring the public who were told that the campaign was not just about raising money but was also a chance for the people of Dundee to show their appreciation for the sacrifices of the RAF and to show both awareness and appreciation of 'what still confronts these heroic fellows'.[9]

One of the key attractions of the week was an RAF exhibition which was to run all week at the Marryat Hall and which was open from 2-8pm on weekdays and from 11am until 8pm on the two Saturdays of the campaign. All of the events such as these helped to bolster the total and the financial institutions and businesses in the city had already pledged large donations, but it was up to the people of Dundee to rally behind them as 'Nothing short of a gigantic effort is now demanded.'[10]

For the Australian airmen who had taken part in the parade to mark the opening of the Wings for Victory week the next day was a sombre one, for it was Anzac Day. At dawn the airmen, escorted by the Dundee Police Pipe Band marched to the top of Dundee Law to take part in a service to the men who fell at Gallipoli in the First World War.

By the end of the second day of the campaign the total stood at £1,953,950 17s 6d and small investors were making contributions, but there was evidence of some anxiety as they were increasingly exhorted to further efforts with 'nothing short of an all-out effort ...

Australian airmen and Dundee police pipe band on Anzac Day. (Dundee Evening Telegraph)

required to reach the record-breaking figure of £4,000,000 which Lord Provost Wilson is anxious that Dundee should contribute'. In order to aid people who could not get to banks during the day the offices of the savings banks had agreed to open every evening during the campaign. Mr Edgar P. Brown and Mr J.B. Thomson of the Savings Committee stressed on 27 April that although people in some areas were responding well to the campaign, others were 'not coming up to the scratch'.

In an effort to encourage, and shame, the recalcitrant the efforts of the city's schoolchildren were held up as an example. Pupils at Hawkhill School, for example, had managed to save an average of £30 per week for the campaign and by the second day had raised the sum of £161. The pupils had adopted the slogan 'Hawks Fly High' as part of their efforts. Other small investors were also held up as an example. In one which was printed in the local press, a street group collector (streets were encouraged to organise collections) called at a savings committee office and handed over a tin box which contained the contents of a collection which had been taken 'by a few bairns about the doors' and told the office staff that she wanted to donate it as a 'tribute to our airmen from the kiddies'. The tin contained small change to the value of 12s 6d.

Another way in which people were encouraged to donate was the promise that they could send a personal message to Hitler by sticking stamps on the 500lb bombs which were on display at Marryat Hall and trust that the RAF would ensure that they were delivered to the correct address in Germany. To illustrate the activities of Bomber Command, the Marryat Hall also showed screenings of a film entitled 'Raid Over Hanover'. Other attractions included a display and explanation of parachute packing by a member of the WRNS. A loudspeaker van was outside in City Square at 4pm with flying officers speaking about their experiences. An RAF Coastal Command band was also booked to play in the Square between 3-7pm. Those who wished to pay the half-crown to climb into the cockpit of the Hurricane which was on display could broadcast a message which would be replied to by a WAAF on duty at Marryat Hall. This final attraction proved very popular and on 26 April almost £10 had been raised by it, particularly from with the members of the ATC.

One suggestion which was made during the Wings for Victory campaign was that a side-fund might be started to separately raise funds for an aircraft which would be named 'Malcolm's Memory' in honour and remembrance of Dundee's first VC of the war, Wing Commander Hugh Malcolm, VC MiD.

The speeches by officers and men of the RAF and Fleet Air Arm in City Square had proved a successful attraction. On the penultimate day of the campaign the main speaker was Flying Officer W. Walton DFC. The fighter pilot had recently returned from Malta and described some of his experiences while on that besieged island. During his time on Malta Flying Officer Walton had been credited with the destruction of six enemy bombers, another three probably destroyed and a further six damaged. The young pilot exhorted his audience to lend their money to the cause as more planes were needed to take the fight to the enemy.

Amongst the groups which were praised for their efforts were the wardens' post 'Matapan' (Post No. 24/3) which had initially set a target of £500 but had in fact raised £1,511, the Co-operative Permanent Building Society which had donated £5,000, and several schools. Liff Road School had raised £212 10s 10d which had exceeded its target of £150. The senior girls, under Miss Young, had raised £7 of this through a variety of works. Ann Street School contributed £706, Rockwell Primary more than £500, and Morgan Academy the sum of £1,337 11s. Rockwell Central School collected £703 in just one week, a remarkable total when it was realised that the average weekly collection at the school was £25. In the week before the schools broke up for Easter this school had donated £105 to the Navy League.

By the end of 1 May the aim for the week-long campaign had been smashed and a total of £3,828,472 had been realised. Provost Wilson wrote to the local press praising the efforts and calling the total a 'splendid tribute to the power of the savings campaign in Dundee'. Despite the total having exceeded the intended target, the Provost still wanted to reach the £4,000,000 mark and urged people to continue donating. In doing so he reminded the people of Dundee that in America the saying was that 'the man that relaxes is helping the Axis' and he concluded that the people of Bonnie Dundee would rise to the occasion. Although the majority of the money had come from large investments it was clear that the people of Dundee had indeed rallied to the cause and small investors received praise for a first-class job.

On 5 May the Wings for Victory campaign was officially closed down and it had indeed exceeded the aim of Provost Wilson and gone beyond £4,000,000. The final tally stood at £4,160,483 5s 7d. This was a remarkable feat for the people of Dundee and attracted widespread praise. The following day the Secretary of State for Air, Sir Archibald Sinclair, sent a telegram to the city offering his congratulations for the magnificent effort of the people of the city and citing them as a great example for the rest of Scotland.

The large numbers of Dundee airmen who lost their lives during the Second World War reflected the fact that many young men saw service in the RAF as more glamorous than other options such as the Royal Navy or Army. It also demonstrates the fact that for significant portions of the war the RAF was the service which was most engaged with the enemy. Bomber Command, in particular, was carrying the war to the enemy on an almost nightly basis and was suffering very heavy casualties as a result. By the evening of 23 May the men of Bomber Command had just enjoyed a very unaccustomed nine-day break from major operations, but on this night some 826 crews were to be sent to bomb Dortmund. The raid was made in good conditions and was very successful although thirty-eight aircraft failed to return. No.57 Squadron at RAF Scampton lost two of its Lancasters on this night. The crew of Sergeant A.R. Leslie, aboard ED970, were shot down by the night fighter ace Major Helmut Lent while over the North Sea. The Lancaster crashed just off the coast and the bodies of three of the seven men aboard were washed ashore. That of Sergeant Alexander Keir Henderson, the 22-year-old wireless operator, was not amongst them. Sergeant Henderson was a Dundee man and had lived at Lochee with his wife, Daisy.[11]

Five days after the raid on Dortmund Harris sent 719 aircraft to bomb the Ruhr town of Wuppertal. This was the outstanding raid of the Battle of the Ruhr with some 1,000 acres of the town being destroyed as well as 71 industrial sites and 1,8000 domestic residences. For this highly successful raid, thirty-three bombers were lost. At RAF Binbrook 460 (RAAF) Squadron lost two of its Lancasters. Sergeant T.P Russell and his crew aboard Lancaster III (W4985, AR-O) were shot down and crashed near Koblenz with five of the crew being killed and the remaining two taken prisoner. The bodies of four of the crew were recovered on 5 June but that of the Dundee-born wireless operator was not found until two days later when his remains were recovered from the Rhine. Sergeant Peter Wright Findlay (22) was buried in the Rheinberg War Cemetery together with the rest of his crew.[12]

The attitude towards Winston Churchill remained ambivalent in Dundee. Many had been impressed by the wartime Prime Minister but there remained a strong undercurrent of bitterness towards him following the decision of the Dundee electorate to vote him out of office as their MP in 1922 and Churchill's subsequent petulant reaction to the defeat. In the summer it was mooted that the freedom of the city be awarded to Churchill and the vote on this reflected this ambivalence. Councillors voted to offer the honour to the PM by sixteen votes to fifteen but Churchill, obviously still bearing a grudge, instantly refused.

Although the risk of enemy bombing was slackening, the Luftwaffe had proved it was still capable of mounting attacks at night and the need for RAF night fighter patrols remained steady. RAF Fighter Command's 29 Squadron had been one of the pioneers of radar-equipped night fighting, but by May 1943 the squadron had been re-equipped with the Mosquito and was able to mount intruder raids over Occupied Europe in addition to patrolling the skies over Britain and this became its main duty. Flying at night in such a high-performance aircraft was never without risk and in the early hours of 21 June the squadron lost one of its aircraft when Mosquito XII (HK169) crashed into the sea off Brightlingsea at 1:40am. Both of the crew were killed. The navigator/radar operator was Pilot Officer James Harvey Petrie, a 21-year-old Dundonian. His remains were washed up and claimed by his parents, James and Elizabeth, and he was cremated at Dundee Crematorium.

On the night of 22/23 June Bomber Command launched a major raid on Mulheim, a medium sized town, which turned out to be highly successful. Industry in the town was badly affected and over 13,700 houses were either destroyed or damaged. Thirty-five aircraft were lost and at least one more Dundee airman had his name added to the long list of the city's dead. Stirling I (EF348, LS-N) of 15 Squadron took off from RAF Mildenhall at 11:38pm with Sergeant J.W. Newport at the controls. While outbound the Stirling was attacked by a night fighter and badly damaged. Sergeant Newport and his crew turned back but were attacked again at 1:30am over the Belgian/Dutch border.

The Stirling was fatally damaged and the crew ordered to bale out as Sergeant Newport attempted to hold the crippled bomber steady. He was killed when the aircraft crashed but five of his crew managed to bale out. The rear gunner, Sergeant Wilfred Chalmers Macaulay, a 21-year-old Dundonian, was also killed. The death of Sergeant Macaulay was particularly tragic as it appeared that he had heard the order to bale out but had become trapped in his turret after his clothing became caught up.[13]

In May and June, General Wladyslaw Sikorski, the Commander-in-Chief of the Polish Army and Prime Minister of the Polish government in exile, had been on an inspection and morale boosting tour of Polish units based in the Middle East. On the night of 4 July, Sikorksi, accompanied by his daughter and a number of British and Polish military officers and dignitaries were on Gibraltar preparing for the final leg of their return to London. The task of conveying the general and his companions fell to 511 Squadron. This was a specialist long-distance transportation unit which operated a variety of aircraft types flying from Britain to the Mediterranean and India. Amongst these was the Consolidated Liberator II (AL532) and its crew, captained by Flight Lieutenant Eduard Prchal, a Czechoslovakian pilot serving in the RAF. The Liberator took off from Gibraltar at 11:07pm but just seconds into the flight Prchal discovered that his elevators had locked and the aircraft crashed into the sea. There were six crew and at least eleven passengers aboard the Liberator but the only survivor was the pilot. One of the crew was Flight Sergeant George Brotchie Robertson Gerry DFM, a 21-year-old from Craigiebank in Dundee, the son of Mr and Mrs Alexander Gerry.[14]

During July there had been several raids on Italy mounted by Bomber Command, but on the night of 16/17 July an experimental raid on a precision target was made. This involved just eighteen Lancasters attacking two transformer stations in northern Italy. The first target was successfully bombed by seven aircraft, but the other target could not be located and an alternative was bombed instead. Two aircraft were lost.

A Lancaster from 467 (RAAF) Squadron crash-landed in North Africa and was burned out (the crew survived) and another Lancaster from 207 Squadron was shot down with the loss of six crew. This was the Lancaster III (DV183, EM-W) of Pilot Officer L.E. Stubbs. The flight engineer in the crew was 33-year-old Sergeant Robert Caven Mitchell, a married father from Dundee. Sergeant Mitchell is buried at Milan War Cemetery where his widow had the following placed upon his headstone: DEARLY BELOVED HUSBAND OF ELIZABETH AND DARLING DADDY OF ROBERT R.I.P.

The night of 9/10 August saw the death of yet another Dundee airman from Bomber Command. On this night 457 aircraft were dispatched to mount an attack on Mannheim. The bombing was scattered due to cloud and poor marking and nine aircraft were lost. Halifax II (JD257, VR-F) crashed at Ludwigshafen, killing all aboard. The flight engineer was Sergeant William Leslie Scott, a 20-year-old former apprentice clerk with Henry Boase & Co. Ltd. The young airman had joined up in May 1941 and was a former member of the 19th (Tay Square Church) Boys' Brigade Company.[15]

On 17 August the crews of Bomber Command were looking forward to a night of rest given that there was almost a full moon, but they were called to the briefing rooms and informed that they were to take part in one of the most unusual raids of the war. The crews of some 596 bombers were to attack the V-2 rocket research facilities on the Baltic island of Peenemünde. The attack consisted of three waves attacking three separate aiming points, guided for the first time, by a master bomber who would orbit the target and give guidance. The attack was a success and the early waves bombed largely unopposed by night fighters, as a diversion to Berlin caught the German controllers out. However, by the time the final wave arrived the German night fighters were over the target and casualties mounted quickly. A total of forty aircraft were lost on this important raid, the majority from 5 and 6 (RCAF) Groups which made up the majority of the last wave. At least three Dundee airmen lost their lives on the operation.

Amongst the aircraft from the final wave which failed to return were four from 61 Squadron at RAF Syerston. Sergeant David Easton was the 20-year-old Dundee-born wireless operator in Lancaster I (W4934, QR-S) which was shot down into the sea, resulting in the deaths of all aboard.[16] No.409 (RCAF) Squadron lost three of its Halifaxes on the operation. Sergeant George Blyth was the flight engineer in Halifax II (JD158, VR-D) which crashed into the Baltic in the vicinity of Stralsund-Gross Zicker. The bodies of four of the crew were recovered but that of 27-year-old Sergeant Blyth, son of Thomas and Eliza Blyth, of Dundee and husband of Annie Blyth, was not amongst them and he is commemorated on the Runnymede Memorial.

Meanwhile 420 (RCAF) Squadron also lost three of its Halifaxes over Peenemünde. Amongst them was Halifax V (EB211, NA-F) piloted by Sergeant J.F. Sheridan, RCAF. The crew were all killed when the bomber crashed into the Baltic and all are buried in the Berlin 1939-1945 War Cemetery. The mid-upper gunner in the crew was Dundee-born Sergeant Norman Rhine Mitchell (20), son of Norman and Marguerite Mitchell. SURE AND STEADFAST was their inscription for his grave.

Late August had seen Bomber Command begin its campaign against the German capital in what became known as the Battle of Berlin. The first raid had occurred on 23/24 August but on the night of 31 August/1 September 622 bombers took off for what the crews referred to as 'the Big City'. There was cloud cover over Berlin and the raid was not a success. Furthermore, German night fighters were highly active over the target and forty-seven aircraft were lost. At RAF Ludford Magna, 101 Squadron lost only one aircraft, but it brought the death of yet another Dundee airman. Sergeant John Findlay was a 35-year-old married man who was serving as the wireless operator in the crew of Flight Sergeant H.G. Edis, RAAF. The crew aboard Lancaster III (JB150, SR-S) were lost without trace and all are commemorated on the Runnymede Memorial.

Casualties in training continued to take its toll of Dundee men who were serving in the RAF. On the night of 23/24 October Sergeant Alexander Robertson was taking part in a night-flying exercise in Whitley V (BD386, ZV-S) of 19 OTU. Something went wrong in the flight and the order to bale out was given. Sergeant Robertson (19), the son of William and Margaret Robertson, managed to successfully bale out but was drowned after he fell into the sea.[17]

The aircraft on the front lines of Bomber Command's war took a battering but many were able to be repaired on site. Before each operation the crew took its assigned aircraft on an air-test to prove its fitness to take part in the forthcoming raid. On 3 November crews were alerted that an operation was to take place (to Düsseldorf) and at RAF Holme in Spalding Moor the crew of Flight Lieutenant J. Steele boarded Halifax V (LK681, MP-A), nicknamed Hetty the Heffulump, to take her up on an air-test. For unknown reasons, however, the Halifax crashed shortly before noon at Enthorpe House, near Market Weighton, Yorkshire. There were only six of the crew aboard (the crew's navigator had stayed behind to prepare his chart for the night's operation) but they were accompanied by a civilian bomb-sight expert, Miss Dorothy Robson, BSc. Flight Lieutenant Steele, his rear gunner, Flight Sergeant H.M. Welch, RCAF, and Miss Robson survived the initial crash, but the rest of the crew were killed instantly. They included the bomb aimer, Flying Officer William Laskie, a 20-year-old from Dundee. His mother, Margaret Chalmers had his body brought home and he was buried at Dundee (Balgay) Cemetery. Flight Lieutenant Steele and Flight Sergeant Welch died the next day and Miss Robson (23) on the following day.

The Battle of Berlin continued to inflict heavy casualties upon the airmen of Bomber Command. On the night of 16/17 December another Dundee pilot lost his life. The command sent 483 Lancasters to the German capital on this night but the Luftwaffe night fighters infiltrated the bomber stream at an early point and some twenty-five Lancasters failed to return. No.576 Squadron at RAF Elsham Wolds lost two on this night. Lancaster I (DV342, UL-G2) took off at 4:27pm but crashed in the target area at Lichtenberg. Only the bodies of the bomb aimer and wireless operator were recovered. The pilot was Flying Officer Ronald Stenhouse McAra, the 22-year-old son of Alexander and Christian McAra of Dundee.[18]

As the bombers returned from the raid on Berlin many of them found their airfields badly affected by low cloud and fog and twenty-nine Lancasters crashed as they tried to get down safely. Amongst the squadrons affected was 405 (RCAF) Squadron at RAF Gransden Lodge. Tragically, the aircraft sent out on the raid had all returned safely but three crashed in England upon return with the loss of fifteen aircrew killed and a further five injured. Lancaster III (JB481, LQ-R) had taken off at 4:37pm with the crew of Flying Officer B. Drew, RCAF, aboard. The bomber came down at 1:30am as it tried to land at RAF Marham in Norfolk. The rear gunner, miraculously, survived without injury but the pilot was badly injured and the remaining five crew were killed. They included the Dundonian flight engineer, Sergeant William Corrigan (28), son of John and Isabella Corrigan, whose body was brought back to his hometown for burial at Dundee (Balgay) Cemetery.[19]

There was another tragedy on 29 December when a Bristol Beaufighter crashed into a wall near to St Andrews while it was being demonstrated. The aircraft, Beaufighter TFX (LZ193) had been delivered to 455 (RNZAF) Squadron just a week previously. Flight Lieutenant William Henry Clemens Toombs, RNZAF, an experienced pilot who had previously served with 489 (RNZAF) Squadron, was demonstrating the flying qualities of the Beaufighter to another pilot when he failed to recover from an intentional low speed stall at low altitude. No.455 Squadron had only just been re-equipped with the type and it seems likely that Flight Lieutenant Toombs had either been transferred or loaned to the squadron to help them get up to speed on the Beaufighter. Flight Lieutenant Toombs was a 25-year-old married man from Christchurch. His body was taken for cremation at Dundee Crematorium (possibly because he had relatives in the area).

1944

The cinema was of huge importance to many during the war; it not only provided entertainment but also Pathé news bulletins. Most, however, visited to take their minds of the bleakness of wartime Britain, with musicals and comedies especially popular. In the first week of the year, for example, the Kings in Dundee was offering its customers 'Stormy Weather' and 'Jitterbugs', starring Laurel and Hardy, while the La Scala was showing 'Stage Door Canteen' and also featured six famous bands. Popular entertainment could be found in the many dancehalls and ballrooms in the Dundee area. Advertised as the largest ballroom in Dundee, The Locarno on Lochee Road gave its customers the chance to dance to first-class swing music and enjoy refreshments in its own café. Dances were held every evening and on Wednesday and Saturday afternoons.

As the invasion of Occupied Europe approached the Allies were aware that the Germans would be watching for signs of where and when the invasion would take place. As a result, the Allies put in place an elaborate deception plan. The main thrust of this diversion took place in England, but Scotland and Dundee also played a role. Operation Fortitude North saw the creation of a fictional army which was poised to invade Norway. To this end, radio traffic and other methods were utilised to intimate that a fictional British VII Corps was headquartered in Dundee along with a real infantry division – the 52nd (Lowland) Division. Operation Fortitude North succeeded in convincing the Germans to retain the 250,000 troops it used to garrison Norway.

The 52nd Division, which had played a role in Operation Fortitude North, was mountain and combined operations trained. It was then switched to the role of an airborne support division. This ambitious plan would have seen the division landed by air along with its own transport but the rapid advance of the Allies in the months following D-Day made the plan redundant.

Advert for The Locarno Ballroom. (Arboath Herald)

At HMS *Condor II*, 751 Naval Air Squadron had been joined by 703 Naval Air Squadron. The station continued to host the two air-sea rescue and reconnaissance squadrons and to provide catapult training for the crews of these units. The transfer of 793 Squadron meant that there were three aircraft being operated from the station. No.751 Squadron continued to operate the Supermarine Walrus, while the newcomers were equipped with both this aircraft and the Vought-Sikorsky Kingfisher floatplane. In May, however, the station was closed and in the following month it was paid off.

It might have been expected that during what was the fifth year of the war the charitable support for the war effort might have become somewhat exhausted, but this does not seem to have been the case. In mid-April the Dundee Savings Bank reported that the first four months of the financial year had seen depositors' balances go up by £539,323, a record and an increase of 10 per cent on the corresponding period in 1943. The balance due to depositors as of the end of March

A Fleet Air Arm Vought-Sikorsky Kingfisher floatplane of 778 Naval Air Squadron at Arbroath. (Public Domain)

A Supermarine Walrus. (Public Domain)

stood at £14,696,315 and the total fund, including reserves, came to a sum in excess of £15,000,000. Clearly, the people and companies of Dundee remained willing to invest their money in the nation's war effort. As a result of this the Dundee Savings Bank announced that it was to invest £100,000 of the special investment department funds in the forthcoming Dundee Salute the Soldier Week which was to run between 22-29 April.

The target set for the Salute the Soldier week was £3,500,000 and the people of Dundee were exhorted to invest whatever they could to reach this total which was to be used to support the 51st (Highland) Division (reformed after its loss in 1940). Even before the campaign began the schoolchildren of Dundee had been urged to save money to invest in the campaign and, to encourage a sense of healthy competitiveness, prizes were to be awarded to the most successful boys and girls. On the opening morning of the campaign Lord Provost Wilson handed out the prizes to the winning boys while his wife handed out the prizes to the successful girls. The Lord Provost roused ringing cheers when he announced that in the past year Dundee schoolchildren had raised £59,245 and that during the war they had raised £175,384. The occasion at which the prizegiving took place was a gathering of 4,000 children at Green's Playhouse where the children had watched a film organised by the Dundee Savings Bank and had a sing-along.

After awarding the prizes the Provost introduced Major General T.G. Rennie, CB MBE DSO, who told the children that he had been fighting with the Highland Division in the desert with many of their relatives and urged them to save as much as they could so that the men of the division could return home as soon as possible.

The campaign was officially opened at noon in a beflagged City Square, in which a Bristol Beaufighter was a focal point. Declaring the campaign open to a large crowd, the Lord Provost said that hc thought the target was achievable and that previous campaigns had exceeded their aims by £500,000 and £1,000,000 respectively and he wanted this year to be a bumper one. Major General Rennie told the crowd that he had been abroad with the Army and had seen British forces in action against the best German troops and he could assure the people of Dundee that there were no finer soldiers than the British. Furthermore, the forces that were gathering in Britain would soon be hurled across the sea to invade occupied Europe and they needed every support that could be given for their maintenance. The Lord Provost then explained how he hoped that small investors in the city would this time exceed the £700,000 which they invested in the previous year. The fact that the invasion was likely to happen in 1944 meant that the people of Dundee were told that their investments had never been more important as the nation faced its greatest test since 1940.

Once again, as was now a familiar tradition, the biggest attraction of the opening day was a parade by representatives of the services. A large crowd watched as the parade, led by the pipes and drums of both the Black Watch and the Argyll and Sutherland Highlanders, marched through the city. The naval contingent included Royal Navy, Fleet Air Arm, WRNS, the allied navies (Free French, Free Dutch and Norwegian), and Sea Cadets. These were followed by the pipe band of Dundee Police, a Royal Engineer Field Company, a Royal Engineer

Bomb Disposal Section, Royal Artillery, Royal Army Service Corps, ATS, three battalions of the Home Guard (accompanied by pipes and drums), the Senior Training Corps (St Andrews University), 1st (Dundee) Cadet Battalion, Dundee High School Cadet Battalion, RAF, WAAF and ATC.

The salute was, on this occasion, taken by Major General Tom Gordon Rennie CB DSO MBE. Major General Rennie had fought in France and had led the 5th Battalion, Black Watch (Royal Highland Regiment) at El Alamein. He went on to command the 154th Infantry Division during the invasion of Sicily before commanding both the 3rd Infantry Division and the 51st (Highland) Division. Towards the end of the war the people of Dundee were saddened to hear that Major General Rennie had been killed in action by mortar fire while commanding the 51st (Highland) Division in Germany.

Major General Rennie taking the salute during the parade to mark the opening of Dundee's Salute the Soldier campaign. (Dundee Evening Telegraph)

A Bofors gun and crew in the parade. (Dundee Evening Telegraph)

Despite the intended and announced target, the organisers hoped that £4,500,000 might be reached. Despite an announcement on the first day that £2,145,350 had already been pledged there were some concerns as this was significantly behind the total for the Wings for Victory campaign of the previous year at such an early stage. Nevertheless, the organisers remained confident that they could still achieve their aim but recognised the magnitude of their task. Once again, the majority of this early total had been donated by various organisations and companies within the city.

Large Early Donations (£10,000 and over) to the Salute the Soldier Campaign:

Investor	Sum
Joint Stock Banks	£1,200,000
Dundee Chamber of Commerce	£256,350
Alliance Trust Co	£200,000
Dundee Savings Bank	£100,000
Dundee Corporation	£50,000
Standard Life Assurance Co	£50,000

Investor	Sum
Scottish Amicable Building Society	£50,000
Anonymous	£25,000
Institute of Art and Technology	£22,000
Royal Liver Friendly Society	£18,000
Dundee Harbour Trust	£10,000
Co-operative Insurance Society	£10,000
Liverpool Victoria Insurance Offices	£10,000
NFU Mutual Insurance Society	£10,000
Dundee, Perth and London Shipping Co	£10,000
Alfred Holt & Co, Liverpool	£10,000
Matador Land and Cattle Co	£10,000
Woolwich Equitable Building Society	£10,000
General Accident	£10,000
Urquhart, Lindsay & Robertson Orcher	£10,000

In the afternoon the Lord Provost presided at an inaugural luncheon at Kidd's Rooms. There was a large company present and they heard the Lord Provost read out an encouraging telegram from the Chancellor of the Exchequer. Recalling the success of previous campaigns, and the fact that the aircraft paid for by the previous year's Wings for Victory week were now pounding the enemy, he told the gathering that the current campaign would allow the city to show its respect for Britain's armies and to help bring the war to a successful conclusion. While acknowledging that money was tighter, he exhorted the city to a great push, saying that it would not do for Dundee to lose the 'peerless reputation of saving and investment which it had gained in the last four years'.

The principal guest at the luncheon was Major General Rennie, a well-known figure in Dundee, having married a Dundee lady whose father was the chairman of the Harbour Board and an industrialist (Mr H. Giles Walker). The general had also found fame due to his surrender at St Valery in 1940 and his subsequent escape. General Rennie said how proud he was to be asked to speak on behalf of the Salute the Soldier campaign and declared that he believed that the Dundee soldiers were amongst the best. He was proud to have served with them in the desert war and in Sicily and of the fact that he belonged to the city's regiment, the Black Watch.

The audience were thrilled with the general's account of the 51st (Highland) Division's campaign in the desert and such battles as El Alamein. He carried his audience through the whole campaign, concluding with the invasion of Sicily. In closing, he said that he wanted to have a word about the soldier. He described how the Army tradition of regimental pride provided the soldier with motivation to fight but that, at the back of every soldier's mind, was the thought of home. He himself liked to think of himself as fighting for his own folk back home and how letters from home meant so much to the average soldier and was his greatest encouragement and inspiration.

The president of the Chamber of Commerce, Mr Alexander J. Stewart, thanked the general and during his speech he remarked that General Rennie had said that the soldier was worthy of their salute, but he wished to reverse the remark and ask if they were worthy of the soldier's sacrifice. Were they were doing enough, giving enough 'to help those fighting fellows in the colossal task which lay before them'? He concluded by saying that it must never come to pass that needless casualties and suffering had been caused by their selfishness in not investing every penny they could.[20]

Even while the Salute the Soldier campaign was ongoing other organisations continued to recruit new members. On the day of the opening of the campaign 1230 (1st Dundee) Squadron, ATC, held an open night in their headquarters at Morgan Academy. The event was organised by the commanding officer of the squadron, Flight Lieutenant A.M. Davie. The cadets gave displays of various skills including navigating in flying kit, signals, aircraft recognition and physical training. One of the highlights was an aircraft recognition quiz between the squadron and an Anti-Aircraft battery with the squadron coming out victorious. The cadets and guests were addressed by the Lord Provost, the Rev J.H. Duncan and the wing commander, Squadron Leader C.N. Ramsay.

The defensive and ARP structures which stood in the city proved a constant attraction to youths and children and sometimes this could lead to dangerous situations. On the night of 22 April four-year-old Albert Soutar, of 20 Hilltown, had a lucky escape. The young lad had climbed the fence surrounding the static water tank in front of the High School and fallen into the tank. Luckily, a passing sailor saw the lad in difficulties and jumped in to rescue him. Both the sailor and the boy were taken to hospital but released that night.

One of the most popular and successful aspects of the various savings campaigns was the groups which formed to collect funds from residents in specific streets. The sense of competition between neighbourhoods resulted in large sums being raised. The residents of one Dundee street had worked out that it cost 5s per mile to run a tank and that it would therefore cost approximately 1,000 times that amount to send a tank all the way to Berlin. They had therefore set themselves the target of raising £250 in order to send a tank all the way to Berlin. This enthusiasm seems to have been typical of the small investors in the city with whom the organisers of the campaign were keen to engage.

Amidst the pomp and ceremony of the grand opening on Saturday 22 April the tellers at the Savings Bank had been exceptionally busy in taking in investments of £27,317. This was their best ever total on the first day of such a campaign and the tellers were equally busy on the second day. The total consisted of £15,664 in excess of savings bond deposits; £5,000 in 2½ per cent savings bonds (1952-1954); £2,828 in national savings certificates and stamps; £2,650 in 3 per cent savings bonds (1960-1970); £1,170 in 3 per cent defence bonds, and £5 in gifts to the Treasury. The banks were able to report that seventy-eight new accounts had been opened on the first day. Despite this encouraging beginning the people of Dundee were still exhorted to even greater efforts. Dundee was the first Scottish city to mount a Salute the Soldier week and the authorities were anxious that a good showing be made. During the second day the people of the city were told that levels of support were below the necessary total and a special effort was needed. The local press said that the start necessitated an SOS to the people of Dundee and urged them to think it over and act upon it. Amongst the donations from large investors on this second day was a further £5,000 to add to the £10,000 which had already been donated by the Dundee Harbour Trustees.

One of the key attractions throughout the Salute the Soldier campaign was the Army exhibition display in the Marryat Hall. So popular was this that the doors to the venue had to be closed at times as the crowds grew too large. The other most popular exhibition was the Beaufighter which stood in City Square. Once again there were a series of talks given in City Square by serving members of the Army. These were led by the official observer from the 51st (Highland) Division, Captain James Borthwick. Bands also played regularly in the square while gramophone records were played over loudspeaker at 10:30am, noon, 3:45pm and 6pm every day.

For Andrew and Jeannie Guthrie of 25 Craigie Street the Salute the Soldier campaign must have been particularly poignant as they received news during it that their only son, Private Stanley David Guthrie (20), was now presumed to have died of wounds on 24 or 25 March 1943. Private Guthrie had been posted missing, presumed wounded, a year previously and the family had been anxiously awaiting further news. A former hammerer at the Caledon Yard, he had joined the Black Watch in May 1939 and was posted out east in July 1941. He had been wounded on two previous occasions.[21]

Dundee had not suffered any serious attempted raids by the Luftwaffe for three years but on the night of 24 April a low-flying enemy aircraft flew over strafing the city with its machine-guns and cannon. Somehow there were no injuries, but many people reported lucky escapes as they fled for cover. The densely populated area around Hilltown and Caldrum

Street was the main focus of the attack and the windows of many tenements and other properties were broken. A cannon shell which had torn a 6-inch hole in the roof was recovered from Henderson's Garage in Strathmartine Road. Twelve days after this attack another lone raider repeated it, flying at roof-top height along High Street as it machine-gunned randomly. Once again, no-one was hurt, but there were recriminations over the manner in which these enemy aircraft had been able to penetrate the air defences around the city.

By the penultimate day of the Salute the Soldier week the £3,500,000 total had been exceeded and still investments poured in, with small savers being markedly enthusiastic. Typical of these was the example of one young Dundee lad. David Burns, of Elmbrae, Westpark Road, was a student at the High School and had recently had a birthday. David had an older brother in the Army and so he called at the Savings Bank and donated his birthday money to the campaign in order to help his brother. This gesture was one of many such examples from the young folk in the city. Works' collections also bolstered the total. Those at W. Fergusson & Sons Ltd and A.C. Wickman Ltd both raised large sums, with the latter investing the sum of £350 in the course of the week. Valentine & Sons Ltd had pledged £2,000 and the works' savings group (which averaged £30-£40 per week) had raised £513 15s during the week. The 'Matapan' wardens' post once again triumphed by breaking their original target. By the penultimate day of the campaign they had raised £2,366 6s 10d and had set a new target of £2,500. Schools had also been heavily involved. Of the big three, Morgan Academy came out on top with £1,835 6d, while second place went to Harris Academy with a total of £1,713 1s 5d and third place to the High School with £1,611 16s 3d.

The City Square continued to be the main focal point of the campaign and many of the displays attracted large crowds. Housewives were particularly interested in the exhibition put on by the Army Catering Corps and the field kitchen demonstration proved a revelation to many. The displays of equipment which were put on by the Royal Engineers also attracted a great deal of attention and positive comment while the various talks by the representative of the 51st Highland Division were also warmly received.

The final day of the campaign saw a meeting held at the Marryat Hall at which the Lord Provost announced that the total raised stood at £3,909,297 8s 6d. Rousing cheers greeted this announcement and there was a great deal of confidence that when the final tally was made Dundee would have smashed the £4,000,000 mark. He reserved special praise for the efforts of the small investors who had contributed £20,000 more than in any other campaign. He related how he had never seen so much money lying on the counters and desks of the Savings Banks, but this was because the safes in all of their branches were full. The Lord Provost also related how he had been anxious in the middle of the week but had been heartened when the Treasurer approached him and told him he was agreeing to double the Corporation's initial investment of £50,000; others, he said, had quickly seen this and followed on.

As Dundee counted the money raised during its massively successful Salute the Soldier week, local families were continuing to receive the dreadful news of the loss of loved ones. One of the roles that was played by the RAF during the war was that of air-sea rescue and a number of specialised squadrons flew in this role, often in scattered detachments around Britain. One of those was 281 Squadron and on 26 April a Dundee airman lost his life on such a rescue flight. Vickers Warwick I (BV409) had been sent to look for survivors at sea just off Puffin Island, Wales. The Warwick and its crew located the survivors and dropped a lifeboat but, as the aircraft circled the lifeboat at low-level to assess the situation, it stalled and crashed into the sea with the loss of the crew, including Flight Sergeant Robert Herbert (31). The son of George and Annie Herbert, Robert had been a pupil at Morgan Academy and a keen and skilful footballer who had played for Elmwood. Prior to joining the RAF he had been employed at the Corporation Transport Department.[22]

The role of the air gunner in the heavy bombers of Bomber Command was a lonely and dangerous one. The mid-upper and rear gunners were separated from the rest of the crew in the rear of the fuselage (they communicated by internal intercom) and were often the first target for an attacking night fighter. On the night of 26/27 April Bomber Command's main raid was on Essen but a second raid made up of 217 aircraft, primarily from 5 Group, was made on Schweinfurt in the south of Germany. Unfortunately, the low-level marking was not successful and poor weather resulted in inaccurate bombing. Once again, enemy night fighters took a toll of the attacking force and twenty-one Lancasters were lost. Three Lancasters from 57 Squadron failed to return to RAF East Kirkby on that night. One had been shot down over Germany, one had collided with another bomber over Germany and the third had been attacked and badly damaged by a night fighter and had made an emergency landing at RAF Tangmere. This Lancaster (ND506) had not only suffered extensive damage, but the rear gunner had been killed and the mid-upper gunner wounded. The victim of the night fighter was 20-year-old Sergeant Alexander Rattray Muir from Lochee. Sergeant Muir had joined up in 1943 and before the war he had been employed by a butcher and had been a member of 6th (Lochee) Company of the Boys' Brigade and a corporal in the Home Guard. His older brother, Charles, a wireless operator in the RAF, was shot down and had been a PoW in Germany for almost two years.[23]

Flight Sergeant Herbert's mother, Annie, of 27 Clepington Road and Sergeant Muir's parents, Alexander and Ann, of 66 Logie Street, both received the news of the death of their sons at the end of the Salute the Soldier week.

By the time the final tally of the money raised during the Salute the Soldier week had been made on 3 May it was found that additional donations had indeed enabled the total to exceed the hoped-for £4,000,000 total with a grand sum of £4,004,427 being announced.

While the Caledon Yard had been building the Castle-class corvettes which had been specially designed to be built by smaller yards, experience had shown the class to be sadly underpowered and production shifted to the larger Loch-class frigates. During the year

An air-sea rescue Vickers Warwick with underslung aerial lifeboat. (Public Domain)

the yard worked on four of these vessels. The first to be launched was HMS *Loch Lomond* which had been laid down in the final month of 1943, launched in June 1944 and was completed in November. HMS *Loch More* was laid down in March 1944, launched in October and completed in February 1945. Two further vessels of this class were worked on during 1994 and launched the following year. These were HMS *Loch Tralaig* and HMS *Loch Arkaig*.

The Castle-class HMS *Hurst Castle* had been commissioned in June but began its working life as a convoy escort in August. The ill-fated corvette did not last long. On 1 September she was part of a search for a German submarine which had been spotted off the northern coast of Ireland by the RAF but at 8:25am the corvette was hit by a torpedo fired by *U-482* and HMS *Hurst Castle* sank in just six minutes with the loss of seventeen of her crew. The 102 survivors were picked up by HMS *Ambuscade*.

In June, Russian Vice-Admiral Levchenko visited the city. This was due to the fact that four former British submarines, HMS *Sunfish, Ursula, Unbroken* and *Unison*, had been handed over to the Russian Navy and they and their crews were being worked up at Dundee.

At the end of August Mrs Catherine Bruce received a telegram at her home at 2 St Matthew Street informing her that her husband, Piper George Bruce (30), had been killed in action in France. Piper Bruce had joined up in 1940 and had served in Iceland before going ashore in France on D-Day with the Black Watch. He had formerly worked at the Wallace Craigie Works on Broughty Ferry Road. For his mother, Jane (of Moncur Crescent), this must have been a particularly bitter blow as she had been widowed in the First World War when Piper Bruce's father

HMS Hurst Castle *on the Firth of Tay after completion.* (Public Domain)

HMS Loch Lomond. (Public Domain)

had been killed while serving as a sergeant in the same regiment as his son. Piper Bruce left behind his widow and two children along with his mother and a brother who was serving in the RAF.[24]

Dundee had escaped remarkably lightly in terms of enemy bombing and most people were now quite relaxed about the prospect of any

 further attacks, but the warning sirens again wailed over the city at 3:55pm on the afternoon of 15 September and many people took to the shelters expecting, perhaps, another lone raider similar to those which had strafed the city earlier in the year. In the event the all-clear sounded at 4:32pm and people emerged from the shelters not knowing that Dundee had just experienced its final alert of the war.

Piper George Bruce. (Dundee Courier)

Bomb disposal team recovering UXB from Taybank Works on Arbroath Street.
(Dundee Evening Telegraph)

Many of the aircrew who served with Bomber Command did not survive to complete their first tour of thirty operations, far less a second tour of twenty or more. Losses in No.8 (Pathfinder) Group were even higher during 1943 and 1944 but some men seemed to lead charmed lives. One such man was Dundee-born Flight Sergeant John J. MacKenzie DFM. The air gunner had been working as a grocer at the Perth Road branch of the Dundee Eastern Co-operative Society before he joined the RAF in 1940. By September 1944 he had completed two operational tours (at least one as a Pathfinder), had flown through the Battle of Berlin and operated on D-Day.[25]

The Red Cross continued its fine work during the year and the annual meeting of the Dundee branch held in October heard that the city had contributed some £34,500 during 1944. This total was higher than the previous year's by more than £5,000. The £22,000 target for the PoWs Parcels Fund had been met and, indeed, exceeded. The committee expressed its especial thanks to the staff at the Yeaman Shore Depot and the organiser, Mr James M. Clark. As the war had progressed, however, more and more Dundee men had been taken prisoner and, as a result, the sum for the next twelve months would be £25,000 in order to pay for the weekly food parcels which were dispatched to Dundee PoWs. Lord Provost Sir Garnet Wilson presided over the meeting and declared that he was very pleased with the work that the branch had undertaken.

The work of the Dundee branch of the Red Cross was very varied and included offering services to injured service personnel who were being treated in the city and to their families when they came to visit. The families of dangerously ill patients, for example, were met upon arrival and accommodation was arranged for them for the duration of their stay. They also provided funds for those Dundee families who wished to visit injured loved ones elsewhere in Britain and by October had provided fifty-three relatives with railway vouchers.

The society also organised the collection of, and payment for, medical supplies. Mrs A. Smith, the supervisor of the surgical dressings department at the Central Depot, reported that some 21,124 articles had been made. These included special dressings for use by the blood transfusion service of the Dundee Royal Infirmary and, in addition, 1,279 items of clothing. The depot organiser at Broughty Ferry, Mrs R.L. Watson, was in charge of overseeing the area's sphagnum moss and hospital comforts supplies. Some 7,949 dressings and 1,295 garments had been made. Sphagnum moss was used in wound dressings because of its absorbent and anti-bacterial properties and was gathered in many rural areas across Scotland and northern England.

During the first two weeks of November the people of Dundee and Angus were denied the pleasure of beef in their meat rations. It had been announced that, due to supply issues, the majority of the meat ration in the area during these weeks was to consist of mutton. Although this was unwelcome news, the press were at pains to encourage people to embrace the matter with stoic resignation and to make the best of it. The *Broughty Ferry Guide and Carnoustie Gazette* of 28 October prepared its readers for this and urged them to accept the ration, adding that it 'should not be difficult for us all to do without beef for a fortnight for we have been one of the best fed of the warring nations'.[26]

On the night of 5 November a well-known Dundee personality died in Dundee Royal Infirmary after a short illness. Hon. Sheriff Substitute John R. Strachan had practised law in the city since 1901 and had been a councillor from 1908-1920. During this time he had been appointed as a magistrate and had served as Provost from 1915 until his retirement in 1920. Born at Macduff in 1877, he had moved to Dundee to join the firm of Boyd & McCrae and later became a partner in the firm of Kilgour, McCrae and Strachan before going to practise on his own in 1915. Despite his burgeoning practice Mr Strachan continued to give his time even after his retirement from the council and served as secretary of the Dundee and District Dairymen's Association from 1923 and was elected president of the Dundee Angling Club in 1936. Mr Strachan was also a keen golfer and a former president of the Dundee Solicitors' Golf Club and a former captain of Scotscraig Golf Club. Living at Tayport, this active man had also served a period as president of Tayport Curling Club. At the start of the war he had been appointed secretary of the local Milk Control Committee. Mr Strachan was survived by his wife and son, Captain J. Stewart Strachan, Royal Artillery.

On the day following the death of Mr Strachan a juvenile court was held at Dundee during which an unnamed 16-year-old Dundee lad appeared charged with five counts of housebreaking. The accused had

Mr John R Strachan. (Dundee Evening Telegraph)

already confessed to the crimes at an earlier hearing and sentencing had been deferred to wait for borstal reports. The crimes had involved the theft of goods to the value of £71 18s 11½d from a house at 3 Robson Street, while others had occurred at 363 Arbroath Road, 21 Loraine Road, 14 Park Road and 28 Strips of Craigie Road. Sheriff Gibb took a dim view of what he told the accused were very serious crimes and sentenced the youth to three years in a borstal.

The cinema remained an incredibly popular form of entertainment and was also a key source of wartime news for many people. In the Dundee area the people had a wide-ranging choice of venue, even in outlying towns. At Broughty Ferry, for example, mid-December saw the Regal offering its customers the musical 'Girl Crazy' starring Mickey Rooney and Judy Garland and the mystery romance 'The Uninvited'. Meanwhile the Picture House was offering its customers Rudyard Kipling's 'Captains Courageous' and 'Henry's Little Secret'. In Carnoustie the Pavilion was showing 'Spotlight Scandals', 'Tiger Fangs', 'Of Mice and Men', and 'The Charge of the Light Brigade', while at the Regal there was 'Mr Muggs Steps Out', 'Danger, Women at Work', 'Women in Bondage', and 'Heaven is Round the Corner'. At Monifieth the Alhambra was offering its customers the murder mystery 'They Met in the Dark' and 'Millions Like Us', a story of an ordinary British family in wartime. In Dundee the La Scala was showing a romantic comedy 'English Without Tears' and the Sherlock Holmes film 'The Scarlet Claw', while the Kinnaird offered 'They Came to a City' and the Kings had 'Song of the Open Road' and 'Eternally Yours'.

Other local entertainments included dancing at a number of venues including the Palace where visitors could dance accompanied by music from Eugene and his Serenaders, while other attractions included the Lido Lovelies, a team of comedy jugglers, a magician and a comedian. The atmosphere at The Empress was a little more refined with dancing and refreshments in the ballroom's own café, while in Broughty Ferry dancers could visit The Chalet.

Above left: *Cinema adverts in the Dundee area over December.* (Broughty Ferry Guide and Carnoustie Advertiser)

Above right: *Cinema and ballroom adverts in the Dundee area over December.* (Broughty Ferry Guide and Carnoustie Advertiser)

CHAPTER 5

1945 – The End in Sight

Although the Clyde had been the main shipbuilding centre in Scotland during the war, Dundee also played its part. During the course of the war the Caledon Yard launched forty large vessels including the convoy escort aircraft carrier, HMS *Activity*. In February HMS *Loch Tralaig* was launched before she was completed in July while HMS *Loch Arkaig* was launched in June but was not completed until November when the war had ended.

By April the war against Germany was obviously reaching its conclusion and many people in Dundee were turning their thoughts towards peace and the future. Others, however, were experiencing grief and loss as they were informed that a loved one had been lost at this very late stage of the war against Germany. Mr Charles Brown and his wife Elizabeth received a telegram at their home at Barry Brae, Barry, informing them that their son had been killed in Germany on 19 April. Guardsman Charles Brown, Scots Guards, was just 19 years old when he lost his life. Prior to joining up in 1943 he had been an apprentice butcher with Messrs D. & A. Winning on Barry High Street. Charles was noted as a particularly bright and popular young man and the local press highlighted the particular tragedy of the notification of his loss having occurred at the same time that all opposition to British troops in Europe had been reported to have ceased. Even more tragically, Guardsman Brown had been home on leave just a week before his death. His parents left this personal inscription on his grave: SACRED TO THE MEMORY OF OUR DEARLY BELOVED SON CHARLES. WE WILL NEVER FORGET.[1]

The late-night broadcast by the government that the war with Germany was over and that the next two days, 8 and 9 May, would be public holidays resulted in some confusion. This meant that the VE-Day celebrations in Dundee got off to a bad start. Many workers did not know whether or not they were expected to turn up for work as usual and the result was chaos on the morning of VE-Day. Large numbers of bewildered workers were seen outside the jute mills, foundries, shops and offices as they turned up for work at the usual time to find that the premises were indeed closed and that the day really was a holiday. Some employers went to the trouble of taking out adverts in the local press informing their workers of the arrangements in place. Baxter Bros & Co Ltd, Dens Works, Eagle Jute Works Ltd, and East Port Works Co., took out a joint advert advising their workers that the firms would reopen on the morning of Thursday 10 May.

At the Caledon Yard around 200 workers turned up only to find the gates locked and they had to make their way home once more. Some foundry workers, however, took matters into their own hands and had paid a late-night visit to their workplace where the night watchman had been able to assure them that the day was to be a holiday. Despite the fact that Dundee Corporation had said it would close down for three days and operate with only a skeleton staff, a number of employees still turned up for work due to the confusion, with many thinking that the holiday would only begin with the formal announcement of peace by the Prime Minister later that day.

Some of the closures had a detrimental effect on the ability of some people to celebrate VE-Day. Outside the Post Office there were angry scenes as pensioners arrived to collect their allowances only to find that the doors were locked and no staff were present. Many of the pensioners expressed their anger that they were going to have to wait until the next day to draw their allowances and many complained that they had been depending upon their pension to provide money for their celebrations.

Large queues also formed outside provisions shops. Bread was a particular concern of many housewives as the basis for many of the street parties was the making of sandwiches and from 8:30am the bakers of Dundee were besieged by hordes of anxious housewives.

Queues also formed outside the butchers' shops in the city but in nowhere near the same numbers.

The news that the war with Germany was over resulted, however, in an outpouring of relief and joy. Streets were decorated with a fabulous display of bunting and flags while some women were dressed in special red, white and blue dresses. The prize for the most well decorated street went to Bernard Street (off Hawkhill), which narrowly beat Overgate. The street was decorated with the flags of all the Allied nations, as well as some yellow flags which puzzled many as to their identity and which turned out to be the defunct flags of the Papal State. The flags were all newly purchased or made and there were no examples of recycled flags from the Coronation, as appeared elsewhere. The decorating of the street was not the main event for the residents of Bernard Street, however. That was to come on the Sunday when every child under fifteen was to be treated to a feast and presented with a shilling.

All of the residents had clubbed together to provide the decorations as well as the food and funds for the celebrations, but the organisers were Mr and Mrs Shepherd of no. 26. This highlighted the ambivalence of many people towards the celebrations, as Mr and Mrs Shepherd were still coping with the anxiety of having a son who was known to be a prisoner of the Japanese. Some residents in Perth Road took an alternative to the more usual displays of flags and bunting and had painted the railings outside their home in red, white and blue.

The YMCA had opened early and was to remain open all day instead of its more regular afternoon hours and it was advertising free meals served all day, as well as a party which was held on the first night of the VE-Day celebrations. The Officers' Club had also scheduled dances for both nights of the celebratory holiday while the British Sailors Club in Nethergate offered free meals throughout the day.

During the morning of 8 May the City Square played host to a large crowd entertained by the Dundee ATC Pipe Band under Pipe Major Angus McLeod. The Polish Military Band was due to play at 2:30pm but heavy rain began shortly beforehand and by 3pm the rain

U2326 surrenders at Dundee 1945. (Dundee Evening Telegraph)

U2326 commander surrendering at Dundee 1945. (Dundee Evening Telegraph)

had become torrential. This dispersed the crowds and put paid to the celebrations which had been planned.

Despite the appalling weather large numbers of young people still braved it to dance and make merry, but the Corporation came in for some criticism for what was seen by some as a lacklustre approach to the organisation of the celebrations. One letter-writer, signing himself as 'Watchman' accepted that it was perhaps too much to expect floodlighting to have been arranged (although it was in many other places) but argued that the Corporation could surely have organised some form of lighting and music for the hundreds of young people who were determined to mark what was the biggest night of their lives with celebration. He concluded that a 'little thought and consideration would have made an awful difference'.[2]

The final day of the victory celebrations saw a turn in the weather as the torrential morning rain turned into a mild and sunny day from midday onwards. Many of the people of Dundee had spent the morning in their homes sheltering from the weather, but as the situation improved, they once more took to the streets and in many locations around the city preparations were begun for the many street parties and bonfires that were to take place.

For football fans the celebrations could not have come at a better time as on the second day of the holiday, Tannadice was to host the second leg of the Forfarshire Cup first round tie between Dundee Utd and Dundee. The first game in the interrupted competition had been played in October at Dens Park and had resulted in a 2-1 win for the home side. People were advised to get to the ground early as it was expected that there would be large queues. In the event some 10,000 fans attended the game which finished in a 1-2 victory for Dundee and saw them progress in the Cup.

In the evening huge crowds packed into City Square as the Polish Military Band played a selection of tunes. The band finished their set at 9pm and some of the older folk began to make their way home but a crowd estimated at 4,000 remained. Music was played through loudspeakers and many of the young people danced through the evening and night. Unlike the celebrations in some other towns, the proceedings in City Square were raucous but orderly. Two sailors attracted cheers and laughter when they took over the platform and danced together. The music stopped at midnight but many of the revellers remained and dancing carried on into the early hours.

In Peddie Street there was a 'non-stop outside variety show' until the early hours as civilians and service personnel danced and sang, accompanied by a variety of instruments including accordions, guitars and drums. The street also had a bonfire and some of the tenants had fixed up their own outdoor electric lights.

In Broughty Ferry the streets were also festooned with flags and bunting. The majority of people were wearing red, white and blue, whether in the form of clothing, scarves or buttonholes, but the heavy rain which developed resulted in quiet scenes across the town. After the Prime Minister's broadcast at lunchtime the church bells rang out across the town. On the evening of VE-Day church services were very well attended. Later, large crowds descended on a dance at the Home Guard Hall. So large was the crowd that revellers came out onto the street and the band was split in two so that everyone had music to accompany their dancing. On the street outside the Corner Hotel an impromptu dance was held.

There was a shortage of flags in some places and many which adorned public buildings were stolen during the night. On the second day of the celebrations the weather improved after a wet start and the main feature of the planned events was the dance held at the Beach Hall in aid of the Welcome Home Fund. The dance had been sponsored by Provost Ruxton and attracted a very large crowd that danced to music supplied by Sharpe's Band. The final evening of the celebrations saw revellers gathered in Gray Street for a dance with music supplied by the BB Pipe Band under Pipe Major Nicholson. Alongside the civilians were many soldiers and land girls and the festivities continued into the early hours after they had moved on to the Lifeboat House. Meanwhile the children of Broughty Ferry enjoyed a number of bonfires which were lit on the beach. On top of one of the largest was an effigy of Hitler and a large crowd gathered to see this spectacle when the bonfire was lit.

In Kirriemuir the second day of celebrations featured a schoolchildren's sports day on the hill with races, five-a-side football and hockey matches, while the evening saw the adults flock to a victory dance in the Town Hall in aid of the Welcome Home Fund which provided funds and comforts for former PoWs who were now returning home. The music was supplied by W. Cameron's Band.

Similar scenes were reflected in every town and village in the arca. Alongside the celebrations, however, were more sombre gatherings as people attended church services to both celebrate the victory and to commemorate those who had lost their lives or had suffered loss as a result of the war. In Monifieth the combined service held in St Rule's Church on VE-Day was very well attended with the members of the town council and their staff being housed in the church's choir and Provost Smith reading the first lesson.

The thoughts of many, however, while overjoyed at the end of the war in Europe were troubled by the fact that a large number of local men were still involved in the fighting with Japanese forces. Others had concerns over loved ones who were known to be prisoners of either the Germans or the Japanese, while the fact that so many local men had lost their lives during the conflict meant that an even greater number of people in the city and its surrounding towns and villages were still grieving the loss of loved ones.

Others were worried about loved ones who were lying in hospital having been wounded at this late stage of the war. Mr and Mrs Keith of 30 Alloway Terrace, for example, had just received the news that their son, Private Frank Keith of the Gordon Highlanders had been wounded in Europe and was in hospital. Private Keith had joined up in 1944 and worked as an apprentice boot repairer before this.[3]

At Broughty Ferry, widowed Caroline Webster McIntyre of 14 Albert Road received the shattering news that her 20-year-old son, Sub-Lieutenant John Alexander Ross McIntyre had been killed while serving in the Far East. In early May the British Pacific Fleet (BPF) was part of operations against Japan and Sub-Lieutenant McIntyre was an observer with 1770 Naval Air Squadron aboard HMS *Indefatigable*. The BPF was, at the time, mounting attacks against airfields on the Sakishima Island as part of the wider campaign against Okinawa (Operation Iceberg). The Japanese air force and naval air forces reacted with great ferocity mounting both conventional and kamikaze attacks on the BPF and its American allies. Several of the BPF vessels, including aircraft carriers were hit. As part of the carrier's air group, 1770 Squadron was tasked largely with flying its Fairey Fireflies in the fighter and fighter bomber roles. Flying against the Japanese in these roles was exceptionally dangerous and Sub-Lieutenant McIntyre failed to return from an operation on 3 May. The young man had been

HMS Indefatigable. (Public Domain)

A Fairey Firefly similar to the type in which Sub-Lt McIntyre lost his life. (RuthAS CCA 3.0)

educated at Dundee High School and started his apprenticeship as a chartered accountant with the firm of Miller, McIntyre & Gellatly of Reform Street, Dundee, before joining up in 1944. He had also been a member of Broughty Ferry's ATC.[4]

The day after the victory holiday saw the city of Dundee return to business as usual with workers turning up dutifully and very few stragglers to be seen from the previous day's entertainments. The manager at one jute mill commented that the two-day holiday had done his employees good and there was a cheerful atmosphere in the mill. The morning saw long queues form once more outside the bakers' shops as people sought to replenish their supplies which had been severely depleted by the two day-long celebrations.

In some places the celebrations had resulted in law-breaking, but in Dundee the celebrants seem to have been remarkably well-behaved. The Sheriff's Court session held on 10 May had no cases from the Police Court as a result of the two-day holiday and Deputy Fiscal

C.F.M. Burrell commented that this was remarkable and extended his congratulations to the people of Dundee for their notable behaviour.

This is not to say that there were no cases at all but those that were heard were unrelated to the celebrations. Amongst them was that of Elizabeth Gracie Crombie (36), care of Mrs Nicoll of 45 Alloway Terrace. Miss Crombie was accused of having stolen a clothing coupon book from 45 Alloway Terrace and having also transferred a book of clothing coupons which belonged to her daughter to a Nellie Watt of 103 King Street, Broughty Ferry, while at the Caledon Yard. Crombie's solicitor explained that his client was employed at the Caledon Yard canteen and she had stolen the book from Mrs Nicholl (with whom she was living) because her daughter was ill and required medicine. She had therefore sold the book containing her daughter's coupons to raise money for the required medicine. Nellie Watt's solicitor added that his client worked with the other accused and had felt sorry for and had thus agreed to buy the coupon book for 32s 6d. Both women admitted the offences and received fines of £5.

On the night of 10 May five Dundee children had a very lucky escape after being found having succumbed to gas poisoning. Mr Patrick Reilly, a munitions worker, returned to his home at 6 Ramsay Street to discover his two sons, James (8) and Hugh (4), his nephew James Reilly (5) and his nieces, Margaret (9) and Mary Reilly (7) unconscious on a bed in the kitchen as a result of coal gas fumes. Fortunately, the children had not been left alone for long and after they were taken to the Dundee Royal Infirmary, they quickly recovered. The source of the leak was a mystery as an inspection showed that the gas fittings were in order and that there was no discernible leak.

Alongside the relief that the war in Europe was over, came the welcome news of the return home of many of the PoWs who had been held by the Germans. Many of these men were brought home quickly as the heavy bombers of RAF Bomber Command joined Transport Command aircraft in ferrying them from airfields in Europe. Amongst those to return home in the days following VE-Day was Warrant Officer

George Ritchie, RAF. The Carnoustie airman had been shot down and captured over Caen in 1941 and had been forced to take part in the long march when German forces marched PoWs ahead of the advance of US forces.

As a result of the speedy return of many men the authorities in Broughty Ferry decided to discontinue collections in aid of the PoWs. The charity had enough funds on hand to maintain supplies of goods for those in captivity in the Far East and agreed to maintain this service until Japan, too, was defeated.

With much of Europe left in ruins and the population of Holland starving there was an immediate requirement for aid. One of the greatest problems was that the transport network in many of the former occupied countries (as well as Germany) had been shattered by the fighting and there was a shortage of both vehicles and petrol. Responding to this crisis the British Road Haulage Organisation sent out an appeal to its members for lorries and volunteers to serve on the continent for a minimum period of six months. In Scotland, it was agreed to send seventy lorries, each one accompanied by a driver and a foreman. Dundee and neighbouring Arbroath agreed to contribute seven lorries to this total and by mid-May the lorries and crews were ready to go as soon as they received the order. For their duties the crews of the lorries had been issued with dark blue battledress uniforms. The Dundee and Arbroath contingent consisted of five lorries from the Dundee firm of David Barrie Ltd and two from Stewart Bros., of Arbroath.

Following the dropping of the atomic bomb on Hiroshima on 8 August, it was increasingly clear that Japan was about to surrender and residents in Marryat Street jumped the gun and held a victory bonfire on the night of 14 August. Fuel for the bonfire was sought out by an eager group of volunteers. One 18-year-old resident let his enthusiasm get the better of him and fell foul of the law. James Lamont of 2 Marryat Street had been asked by the organisers of the fire to gather some fuel. He had gone to an air raid shelter in the playground of St Martin's Episcopal

Volunteer lorry crews for European aid mission. (Dundee Evening Telegraph)

School on Caird Avenue and kicked open the door before stealing three wooden forms which were then used to stoke the bonfire. Following a complaint and subsequent investigation Mr Lamont was arrested. He was no stranger to trouble having been convicted three times and he was a deserter from the Army. He appeared in court on 21 August and was fined £3 by Honorary Sheriff Substitute James Fenton. The Hon. Sheriff said that he had been lenient after making allowances for the circumstances and exuberance at the end of the war.

The announcement that Japan had surrendered came at midnight on the night of 14/15 August and, although it had been anticipated for some time, many Dundee folk were in bed when the news came. They were very quickly made aware of the end of the war as a barrage of noises awoke them. Rockets flared into the sky from the ships moored on the Firth while sirens wailed out the V-sign and, very speedily, bagpipes and accordions were brought out onto the streets as impromptu parties began. Just half an hour after midnight City Square was packed with people, many of whom were dancing merrily. The first to arrive had been five sailors who immediately tore down a Japan exhibition banner and draped it over a savings campaign poster. All across the city, people flocked to the celebrations as the news spread. Many of these impromptu processions were led by pipers and accordionists and many travellers who had been making for the last trams took the decision to stay behind and enjoy the festivities. Fireworks were periodically set off while the beacon at the war memorial on Dundee Law was lit up. At least one large bonfire, at Maitland Street, was lit. By breakfast the flags and bunting of VE-Day had reappeared, although not in quite the same numbers as in May.

With 15-16 August marked as national holidays in the same way as for VE-Day the preparations began once more for parties, although the celebrations were on a slightly lower key than the previous occasion. Once again, very large queues developed outside shops with bakers being particularly impacted. Outside most bakers the queuing had begun at 6:30am and many people stood outside in the inclement weather for a considerable time before bread supplies arrived. Once again, the Corporation came in for some criticism of its apparent slowness to react and the many people who went to City Square were met with the sight of an empty platform which was not decorated until that afternoon. One city centre fruiterer had managed to obtain a supply of grapefruit and this attracted a queue hundreds of yards long.

Many church services were held and bells rang out intermittently throughout the day. One of the most moving services was held at Dundee Law where the acting Provost, Bailie Drummond, accompanied by other members of the Corporation, laid a wreath on the memorial. Elsewhere, workers from the Gas Department could be observed working feverishly to put in place floodlighting at the High School and Broughty Castle. Other sites to be floodlit included the City Square, the War Memorial and many of the city's churches.

Throughout the morning the various service cafes and canteens were making preparations to provide meals over the two-day festivities. The YMCA had, once again, decided to offer free meals all day and had extended this to the canteen which it ran at Tay Bridge Station. Entertainment had been planned for the afternoons of both days and on the second day the YM Canteen was hosting a three-course special celebratory lunch. At Holland House a joint Dutch/Scottish dance was being prepared. The dance began at 5pm and went on until 11pm. A *Thé dansant* was also planned for the following day. One Dutch sailor who visited the canteen on the morning of VJ-day related how he had only been in Britain for a month having been rescued by US forces after being a prisoner of the Germans for four years. During this time he had been sentenced to death for attempting to escape to Britain, but was freed before the sentence could be carried out. The Sailors' Club in the Nethergate also threw open its doors with a wide latitude being given to the nature of visitors who were brought there by the promise of a free meal and the impromptu sing-songs maintained throughout the day. The Officers' Club on Reform Street planned dances for both nights of the VJ-Day celebrations.

Despite the heavy rain in the afternoon, large crowds gathered in City Square to be entertained and dance to music from the Boys' Brigade bands. By mid-afternoon the crowds in City Square had swelled to 5,000 or so and overspilled onto High Street and the Caird Hall Steps.

Many people also attended the thanksgiving service held at St Mary's (Dundee Parish) Church including the acting Provost, the Chief Constable and many other members of the Corporation and other dignitaries. The Rev Henry M. Bartlett urged the congregation to ensure that they dedicate themselves to making the vision of those who had fought a reality. The development of the atomic bomb had made it more urgent than ever before that the world unite in peace.

The night of 15 August saw mass celebrations as Dundee folk turned out *en-masse*. The Corporation Transport Department reported that it had faced its busiest night ever, with the period between 9:45-11:30pm being particularly busy. Exceptional queues built up for buses and trams and many people missed the final trams and had to walk home. The bus stand at Shore Terrace put on fifteen special buses in order to cope with the 10,000 people who passed through. This was despite the fact that there was, once again, torrential rain.

The following morning saw massive queues outside many shops, particularly bakers, as housewives grew anxious about feeding families over a two days' holiday followed by a weekend. Many of those out and about took the opportunity to listen to the music which was played in City Square throughout the morning. At 3pm the weather began to clear somewhat and a crowd of approximately 3,000 gathered in City Square to listen to the City of Dundee Pipe Band. Bernard Street, winner of the best-dressed street on VE-Day drew many sightseers. The residents, aware that victory was approaching, had begun putting their flags and bunting out on Sunday 12 August and the display was said to be even better as more flags and bunting had been purchased since VE-Day. Dominating the display were portraits of Attlee, Stalin, Truman and Chiang Kai-Shek, along with a composite flag representing the nations of Great Britain, the USA, Russia and China. Many visitors put money in a collection tin for the Bernard Street Welcome Home Fund. The street had ninety-three residents away in the forces. Of these four had been killed and four demobbed. Several dances and other events were planned for the night and landmarks were to be floodlit.

VE Day celebrations in Bernard Street 1945. (Dundee Evening Telegraph)

In Carnoustie it seemed that many young people had taken to the streets within minutes of the midnight announcement. Singing and cheering resounded through the town as the crowds paraded down High Street and Dundee Street. Motor vehicles drove along the roads sounding their horns. Someone managed to open up the Beach Hall and a pianist was quickly found, whereupon an impromptu dance began, continuing until 4am. The flags once again appeared in the streets and large queues once again formed outside many shops with fish shops and bakers bearing the brunt of the demand. Many housewives had been caught by surprise and there was some desperation to lay in sufficient supplies for the festive holiday and the following weekend. Rain began at around 2pm and grew steadily heavier until it was a deluge which washed out all plans for outdoor activities. An outdoor band and dance had to be abandoned and many of the young people were angry when they found out that the Beach Hall had been booked for a private dance. Thus, dancing for most was confined to the Beach Tea Room where the proprietor gave a warm welcome to the large crowds who assembled there. Despite the rain, the bonfire was lit at 9pm and the crowds braved the weather to see the bonfire and firework display.

On the following day the children's sand-castle competition was held with over sixty competitors taking part. The winners were Ann Paton (under 6s); Ian Barclay (7-9); Charles Scobie (10+). In the afternoon the members of the Burgh Band led a fancy-dress parade to the Beach Hall, which was packed with spectators. There were over 100 contestants and the winners were Patricia Robertson (under 6s); Aileen Patterson (7-9); and Ian Laurie and Dusty Millar (10+). The festivities were concluded with dancing and a fireworks display.

The celebrations at Monifieth were also ruined by the rain with a dance and several bands being cancelled as a result of the weather. In the morning, the members of Monifieth Town Council attended a wreath laying ceremony where Provost Smith laid the wreath before attending a combined church service at St Rules. Despite the rain, the bonfires on the foreshore did go ahead.

The Caledon Yard had a proud record during the war. We have already heard of some of the warships and merchant vessels which were constructed there. Much of the work undertaken, however, was the refitting of vessels. From 1942–1944 there was always at least one escort carrier being refitted in Dundee. This had begun with the refit of HMS *Biter*, the largest of her class, but had been a valuable wartime service. From March 1940, when the refit of the destroyer HMS *Jaguar* was undertaken, the yard was almost constantly refitting naval vessels. In the course of the war a grand total of 198 Admiralty and Allied ships were refitted at the yard. This work was maintained even while new ships were being constructed.

Dundee had not seen the bombing which some had expected and the city could be said to have escaped lightly, but many Dundonians had made the ultimate sacrifice during the war with people in all three services making a substantial contribution to the war effort. The loss of the 51st (Highland) Division came as a bitter early blow and resulted in a large number of local men being held as PoWs for almost five years. Elsewhere the Dundee sailors of the Royal Navy and Merchant Navy made a worthy contribution and paid a high price, while the local airmen paid a huge price in terms of lives lost. The city's industries had also made a significant contribution but, like older industries in other cities across parts of northern Britain, faced a very uncertain peacetime future.

From 1939-1945 at least 1,880 Dundonians lost their lives. The worst single year for Dundonian casualties was 1944 when at least 494 were killed. Of those in the three services the average age of the losses was just 26. The average age of the losses in the Merchant Navy was 34 and of civilians 42. For those interested in analysing the Dundee casualties of the war the Leisure and Culture, Dundee, website has an excellent database at:

http://www.leisureandculturedundee.com/roh/infostats.htm.

This resource can be of great use to anyone wishing to further research Dundee casualties during the war.

As had been said in numerous speeches made on VE and VJ-Day, it was now up to those who had lived through the war to ensure that the people of Dundee enjoyed a profitable, peaceful and happy future.

Endnotes

Chapter 1: 1939 – Dundee at War

1. *Dundee Courier*, 12 September 1939, p.3.

Chapter 2: 1940 – ARP, LDV and Home Guard

1. *Dundee Evening Telegraph*
2. *Dundee Evening Telegraph*, 2 January 1940, p.2.
3. *The Scotsman*, 5 January 1940, p.7.
4. Following this very eventful and important service the SS *Arbroath* returned to merchant service and led a long life, being scrapped in Ireland in 1972.
5. *Dundee Courier*, 3 February 1940, p.4.
6. *Broughty Ferry Guide and Advertiser*, 25 May 1940, p.5.
7. *Dundee Courier*, 24 June 1940, p.4.
8. *Ibid*.
9. Sgt Main's body was brought back for cremation in his home city.
10. P/O Dickie has no known grave and is commemorated on the Runnymede Memorial.
11. *Dundee Courier*, 2 August 1940, p.4.
12. *Dundee Courier*, 3 August 1940, p.4.
13. Lance Corporal Vaughan is buried at St Valery-en-Caux Franco-British Cemetery.

Chapter 3: 1941–1942 – A Long Struggle

1. *Sunday Post*, 9 February 1941, p.20.
2. *Dundee Courier*, 11 June 1941, p.2.

3. *Ibid*.

4. *Dundee Evening Telegraph*, 11 June 1941, p.5.

5. *Dundee Courier*, 22 October 1941, p.3.

6. Sgt Blacklaw was brought home for burial at Dundee Eastern Necropolis. The Hurricane pilot was also killed in the tragic accident.

7. Sergeant Fyfe is commemorated on the Runnymede Memorial.

8. P/O Henderson is buried at Rheinberg War Cemetery.

9. The all-RAF crew in this RCAF squadron were: Sergeant E. Harrison (pilot); Sergeant J.S. Gething (observer); Sergeant L.C. Nall (wireless operator/air gunner) and Sergeant G.J. Laing (wireless operator/air gunner). Sergeant Nall survived to be taken prisoner while the others are buried at Guidel Communal Cemetery.

10. The crew were: F/O J.B. Munro, RNZAF (pilot); F/O G.R. Lind, RAAF (observer); F/Sgt J. Storey, RAF (wireless operator/air gunner); P/O I.P. Clark, RAF (wireless operator/air gunner); and Sgt H.H. Hudson, RAF (air gunner). F/O Lind has no known grave and is commemorated on the Runnymede Memorial while the other men are buried at Westerschelling General Cemetery.

11. P/O Morris-Edwards is buried at Stok-on-Trent (Fenton) Cemetery.

12. Senior 4th Engineer Wilson is commemorated on the Tower Hill Memorial.

13. Leading Steward Christison is commemorated on the Chatham Naval Memorial.

14. Wing Commander Malcolm, VC, was buried along with his crew at Beja War Cemetery. The crew were: W/Cdr H.G. Malcolm, VC, MiD (pilot); F/O J. Robb (navigator); and P/O J. Grant, DFC (air gunner).

Chapter 4: 1943–1944 – The Turn of the Tide

1. The crew were: Sgt E.B. Withell, RNZAF (pilot); Sgt J.S. Hunter, RAF (flight engineer); F/Sgt W.G. Burrow, RAAF (navigator); F/Sgt A.F. Neale, RAAF (bomb aimer); Sgt R.B. Mullinger, RAAF (wireless operator); Sgt A. Mitchell, RAF (air gunner); and Sgt L.H. Richardson, RAF (air gunner).

2. Sgt Ross is commemorated on the Runnymede Memorial.

3. The 379 dead represented the second worst loss of life in a naval incident in home waters (second only to that of HMS *Royal Oak*). Survivors were ordered not to talk about the event. In 1999 boards from the flightdeck of HMS *Dasher* washed up on the coast at Ardrossan and an archaeological dig took place in 2012 at Ardrossan Cemetery, but no evidence of the mass grave was discovered in the area covered. It has been postulated that one of the corpses from HMS *Dasher* was the one used in the deception plan codenamed Operation Mincemeat.

4. In 1946 HMS *Activity* was sold into merchant service as the MV *Breconshire*. She was scrapped in 1967.

5. Sergeant Milne and his crew are buried at Hamburg Cemetery.

6. Sgt Andrew and his crew are commemorated on the Runnymede Memorial.

7. Pvt Keir is buried at Sfax War Cemetery.

8. Sgt Webb and his crew are buried at Rheinberg War Cemetery.

9. *Dundee Courier*, 22 April 1943, p.3.

10. *Ibid.*

11. The all-RAF crew were: Sgt A.R. Leslie (pilot); Sgt H. Kleiner (flight engineer); P/O J.R. Morton (navigator); Sgt P. Hemingway (bomb aimer); Sgt A.K. Henderson (wireless operator); Sgt W.J. Bennett (air gunner); and Sgt P. Daly (air gunner). Sgt Kleiner is buried at Leeuwarden Jewish Cemetery while the two air gunners are buried at Terschelling and Ameland respectively. The remaining crew are commemorated on the Runnymede Memorial.

12. The crew were: Sgt T.P. Russell, RAF (pilot); Sgt W.F.C. Clague, RAF (flight engineer); Sgt R.W. Dunn, RAAF (navigator); Sgt T. Taylor, RAAF (bomb aimer); Sgt P.W. Findlay, RAF (wireless operator); Sgt D.B. Gordon, RAF (air gunner); and Sgt G.A. Kirk, RAAF (air gunner). Sgt's Dunn and Kirk survived.

13. Sgt Macaulay and his pilot are buried at Heverlee War Cemetery. Two of the crew managed to evade capture while the remaining three were taken prisoner.

14. Included amongst the dead passengers were Colonel Victor Cazalet, MC, the British liaison to the Polish forces and Brigadier John Percival Whiteley, OBE, the Conservative MP for Buckingham. The crash continues to cause controversy and has given rise to a number of conspiracy theories which state that Sikorski was the victim of an assassination. Evidence is extremely sketchy and many documents are still secret but testimony received thus far simply implies an unexplained mechanical fault. F/Sgt Gerry's body was one of several which were never recovered and he is commemorated on the Gibraltar Memorial.

15. Sgt Scott is buried with his crew at Durnbach War Cemetery. Sgt Scott was the only RAF airman in this otherwise all-RCAF crew which consisted of: F/O N.T.R. Ludlow (pilot), Sgt W.L. Scott (flight engineer); P/O C.A. Wright (navigator); Sgt A.S. MacLaren (bomb aimer); Sgt C.R. Smyth (wireless operator); Sgt D.R. See (air gunner); and Sgt W.D de Molitor (air gunner). The average age of the crew was just 22.

16. The crew were: F/O W. Hughes (pilot); Sgt T. Graham (flight engineer); Sgt L.H. Scholey (navigator); Sgt B.J.W. Brown (bomb aimer); Sgt D. Easton (wireless operator); Sgt R.C. Walton (air gunner); and Sgt W.B. Ness, RCAF (air gunner). The bodies of Sgt's Graham and Ness were washed ashore and buried at Swindemunde while the others are commemorated on the Runnymede Memorial although subsequent investigations have revealed that the body of Sgt Brown lies in Berlin 1939-1945 War Cemetery.

17. Sgt Robertson is commemorated on the Runnymede Memorial.

18. F/O McAra is commemorated on the Runnymede Memorial.

19. The crew was: F/O E.B. Drew, RCAF (pilot); Sgt W. Corrigan, RAF (flight engineer); F/Sgt V. Mienert, RCAF (navigator); F/Sgt H.M. Saunders, RCAF (bomb aimer); W/O2 W.L. Dobson, RCAF (wireless operator); Sgt H.R. Bessent, RCAF (air gunner); and Sgt L.A. McCrea, RCAF (air gunner). Sgt McCrea survived but F/O Drew died of his injuries on 28 December. At just 18 years of age

Sgt Bessent was amongst the youngest RCAF airmen to lose his life with Bomber Command.

20. *Dundee Courier*, 22 April 1944, p.2.
21. Pvt Guthrie is buried at Medjez-el-Bab War Cemetery.
22. F/Sgt Herbert is commemorated on the Runnymede Memorial.
23. Sgt Muir is buried at Dundee (Balgay) Cemetery. The wounded mid-upper gunner, Sgt Allen Hdson survived the war. The rest of Sgt Muir's crew, with two replacement gunners, were all lost on 22nd June 1944 during a raid on Wesseling. They were: F/Lt R.A.W. Beaumont, DFC (pilot); F/S M.A. Clark (flight engineer); P/O D.J. McCrudden (navigator); WO2 T.H. Mayne (bomb aimer); W/O C.H.T. Hurley (wireless operator); F/Sgt G.R. Ansdell (air gunner); and F/Sgt E.H Goehring, RCAF (air gunner).
24. Piper Bruce is buried at Bayeux War Cemetery.
25. F/Sgt MacKenzie survived the war.
26. *Broughty Ferry Guide and Carnoustie Gazette*, 28 October 1944, p 4.

Chapter 5: 1945 – The End in Sight

1. Guardsman Brown is buried at Becklingen War Cemeterry.
2. *Dundee Courier*, 10 May 1945, p.2.
3. Pvt Keith survived his wounds.
4. Sub-Lt McIntyre is commemorated on the Lee-on-Solent Memorial.

Index